Role Play in the Early Years

Pirates

and other adventures

Related titles of interest:

Drama Lessons for Five to Eleven-Year-Olds
Judith Ackroyd and Jo Boulton
1 85346 739 1

Beginning Drama 4–11, 2nd edition
Joe Winston and Miles Tandy
1 85346 702 2

Planning Children's Play and Learning in the Foundation Stage
Jane Drake
1 85346 752 9

Role Play in the Foundation Stage
Sue Rogers
1 85346 963 7

Outdoor Play in the Early Years
Helen Bilton
1 85346 952 1

Other titles in the series:

The Teddy Bears' Picnic and other stories
Jo Boulton and Judith Ackroyd
1 84312 123 9

The Toymaker's Workshop and other tales
Jo Boulton and Judith Ackroyd
1 84312 125 5

Role Play in the Early Years

Pirates
and other adventures

Jo Boulton and Judith Ackroyd

Drama Activities
for 3–7 year olds:

Book 2

🐇 David Fulton Publishers

David Fulton Publishers Ltd
The Chiswick Centre, 414 Chiswick High Road, London W4 5TF

www.fultonpublishers.co.uk

First published in Great Britain in 2004 by David Fulton Publishers

10 9 8 7 6 5 4 3 2 1

Note: The right of Jo Boulton and Judith Ackroyd to be identified as the authors of this work has been asserted by them in accordance with the Copyright, Designs and Patents Act 1988.

David Fulton Publishers is a division of Granada Learning Limited, part of ITV plc.

Copyright © Jo Boulton and Judith Ackroyd 2004

British Library Cataloguing in Publication Data
A catalogue record for this book is available from the British Library.

ISBN 1-84312-124-7

Typeset by FiSH Books, London
Printed and bound in Great Britain

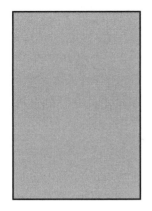

Contents

For the boys in our lives
The Andys, Charlie, Toby and Rupert

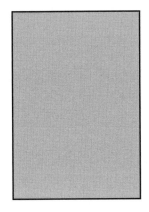

Acknowledgements

We would like to thank the students and teachers who have tried out these materials. We are especially grateful to Paula Pearce, Roz Conlon and Perry Hall for their stories from the classroom. The support and friendship of colleagues in Education and Performance Studies at University College Northampton is valued and appreciated.

Over the years the work of Dorothy Heathcote, Gavin Bolton, Cecily O'Neill, David Davis and Jonothan Neelands has influenced our practice. We are grateful for their pioneering contributions to the field and their inspiration. Warm thanks to David Booth for his contagious enthusiasm for children's stories.

Thanks also to Nina Stibbe at David Fulton Publishers for asking us to write this series. We appreciate the enthusiasm and careful attention of Nina, Paul, Alan and their colleagues throughout the process.

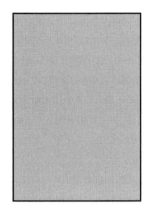

Introduction

There's something empowering for young children about drama.
It's about learning and problem-solving in their world.

We share teacher Angie Matthews' enthusiasm about using drama with young children and have therefore designed this series of three books to encourage a wider use of drama in early years settings. The series is designed to support those unfamiliar with drama activity as well as to offer experienced teachers a range of new materials.

Many teachers feel anxious about doing drama, but the fact is that teaching drama can no longer be avoided, no matter how scary it may seem. All children have a statutory entitlement to engage in dramatic activity. Drama is featured in the *Curriculum Guidance for the Foundation Stage* where children are required, for example, to *Use language to imagine and recreate roles and experiences* (DfEE/QCA, 2000: 58). Similarly in the National Curriculum, at Key Stage 1 drama activities are highlighted. For example, pupils must learn to

- use language and actions to explore and convey situations, characters and emotions;
- create and sustain roles individually and when working with others;
- comment constructively on drama they have watched or in which they have taken part.

(DfEE/QCA, 2000: 44)

The *National Literacy Strategy Framework for Teaching* makes explicit reference to drama. In Year 1 Term 1, for example, children will *re-enact stories in a variety of ways, e.g. through role play, using dolls or puppets* (DfEE, 1998: 20). Indeed, drama is an interactive and exciting teaching strategy which, by its very nature, illuminates the possibilities for interrelating the three language modes of speaking and listening, reading and writing.

While drama offers contexts and possibilities for development in aspects of English, it also provides a plethora of other learning opportunities at the same time. Thus while children are using persuasive language, they may also be considering the fragility of the environment. In addition, they may also be developing skills in group work and citizenship all at the same time – through involvement in the same one dramatic activity!

Many teachers are expected to use drama activities with little or no relevant training, often resulting in a lack of both confidence in and understanding of educational drama practice. Student teachers, early years practitioners in Foundation Stage settings and teachers in Key Stage 1 classrooms have regularly asked us for drama ideas they can try that will work with their children. The dramas in this series have been tried and tested by teachers new to drama and also by experienced practitioners. They have found these activities valuable in themselves and also useful as a springboard for developing their own ideas.

There is no doubt that early years practitioners recognise the pedagogic value of children's play. Home corners, imaginative play areas, pretend corners (call them what you will) have been a regular and exciting feature of the early years setting. There are a number of texts available offering ideas and advice on setting up such environments. The activities offered in this series, however, focus on ways that the adult can work in role alongside the children to enhance learning opportunities. Teacher involvement is crucial. Here it is not only the children who enter imaginative worlds but the children and their teacher who create and explore these fictional worlds together. This approach, namely the teacher in role, enables the teacher to work with the children from inside the drama. The teacher in role can structure the children's contributions, provide stimulating challenges and create appropriate atmospheres. The teacher in role creates situations that demand of the children particular language skills, understanding and empathy. The teacher in role provides a model of commitment to working in role that children can follow.

This book contains a range of drama teaching ideas organised into chapters. In each chapter two types of activity are presented. The drama activities are presented in the body of the page, and non-drama activities, such as reading or music, are presented in circles. The layout of the activities offers practitioners the possibility of finding their own pathways through the material, which are appropriate to their own teaching context. This flexible approach enables pathways through the material to be selected according to a range of possible factors: the chosen learning objectives; knowledge of the children's needs; the space and time available; the level of teacher confidence, and perhaps the time of year or geographical locality or local events. The three teachers' stories of 'Jack and the Beanstalk', a drama from this book, demonstrate how they found their own pathways and different emphases. General aims for the chapters are provided, along with suggestions for resources. Each drama activity indicates possible teacher intentions to make clear the dramatic process. The relevance of each of the dramas to the National Curriculum and Early Learning Goals is set out at the end of the book.

In Book 1 in this series, *The Teddy Bears' Picnic and other stories*, we have included the transcript of a teaching session of 'The Park', a lesson in Book 1. This is not to invite you to replicate the way it was done in this instance, but to give you an idea of how drama occurs in the classroom as opposed to how it appears in a book. It illustrates how a teacher can respond to what the children bring and to the moments when they do not contribute. It is an honest, straightforward account of a drama-teaching experience with the words of both teacher and children.

The following chapters will help teachers to create a range of imaginary contexts in which children will encounter weird and wonderful, noble and naïve, wicked and whimsical characters.

Sarah Hudson taught her first ever drama lesson using one of these chapters. She writes:

Without wanting to sound too nauseating and over the top, I would say that this afternoon was one of the most rewarding I have had the pleasure of sharing with my class. It has definitely inspired me to continue to share drama activities with my class. If a novice, or definitely a non-expert, could manage this with such success, then I am sure anyone could.

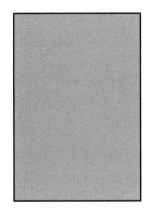

How to use this book

Where do I begin if I have never done drama before?

Looking at 'Jack and the Beanstalk' (Chapter 4) and then at 'Stories from the classroom' will give you a sense of how these dramas work and what is required of you. It is probably best to follow the activities step by step when you begin to use drama. You will soon want to add your own ideas. Book 1 of the series includes a transcript of a drama to get a feel of what might take place. It includes what was said by the children and teacher. Reading this may be helpful to those who are completely new to drama.

Do the dramas fulfil any National Curriculum objectives or Early Learning Goals?

Yes. All the dramas provide the possibility of covering a very wide range of Early Learning Goals (ELGs) and National Curriculum (NC) objectives, as you will see at the back of the book. You may choose to focus on specific objectives which may be most appropriate to your children and their needs.

How many children do I work with?

These dramas have been designed for use with any number of children between four and thirty.

How long do the dramas take?

You need to consider how long you have and how long you wish to give to the activities. We recommend a maximum of thirty minutes with children in the Foundation Stage. However, we have sometimes lost track of time and found that we have been working for much longer. You need to gauge the children's response.

You may choose to teach just one activity and then pick up the story again another time. You can do a drama in one session or over a week.

What initial information is provided?

- Each chapter is laid out with an introduction telling the story of the drama.
- The overall aims of the drama are then provided which concern both drama and other curriculum areas.

- Key themes are listed.
- Resources are listed. These are usually optional, but any essential items are indicated. Some resources have been included, such as the treasure map for the 'Pirate Adventure'.
- Also provided are suggestions for imaginative play areas.

How are the activities explained?

- Drama and non-drama activities are provided. The non-drama activities are presented in circles at the side of the page.
- Teacher's intentions for each activity are listed. These pertain to the thinking behind the particular activity described. Headings provide an indication of both the type of dramatic activity (e.g. 'Whole class improvisation') and the content (e.g. 'Creeping into the giant's house').
- *Italics* are used to distinguish direct speech and explanation. The direct speech provides suggestions of what the teacher might say and examples of what children have said during the drama.
- Clear explanations of drama terminology used in the chapters are included in the 'Glossary'.
- A number of generic games used in the dramas are also described in detail.

Do I have to follow the plan?

No! It is important that you read through the materials to familiarise yourself with the story. You can then make choices about your own pathway through the materials. In the 'Stories from the classroom' we see that Perry chose to do some additional thought bubble activities when teaching 'Jack and the Beanstalk', and Roz added some dance. Paula responded to the children's requests to change the way the thought tunnel was organised. The plans can be followed as they are laid out, or you can select which activities you wish to use depending on your experience, your context and your children. You can make the dramas your own as Paula, Roz and Perry have done.

Do I have to use teacher in role?

Yes. All of these dramas include teacher in role to some degree. The rationale behind this series of books is based upon the teacher working in role from inside the fiction alongside the children. However, this does not mean that you have to use exaggerated voices and walks. You are not required to wear a costume or use props, although we provide suggestions of what might be used to help young children distinguish between you as teacher and you in role. It is important that you make it very clear when you are in role to avoid confusion. A hat is often easy to put on and take off as you move between teacher and role.

How do I use an imaginative play area?

Imaginative play areas may be set up by the teacher and children together. They provide a context for the dramas. This does not mean to say that you have to do the drama in the imaginative play area. If you are working with a large group, there won't be room. In this case, you can refer to the imaginative play area as if it is your backdrop.

Suggestions for how you might create such areas are provided in the chapters. All the dramas may be taught without imaginative play areas. If you are working in a large space, such as a school hall, we strongly recommend that a corner is cordoned off because too much space can lead to difficulties.

Stories from the classroom

Jack and the Beanstalk

We asked three local teachers to write stories about their experiences of using 'Jack and the Beanstalk' (Chapter 4) with their classes. Paula is a second-year English specialist BAQTS student who taught 'Jack and the Beanstalk' as her very first drama lesson. Roz is a freelance dancer studying on an Applied Arts MA course. She had never used teacher in role before, *'but it's quite fun, isn't it!'* Perry has been using some drama in his teaching over the past ten years. Reading their stories may help you to conceptualise how the teaching materials are transported from page to practice. The children's names have been changed.

▌Paula Pearce's story
▌Grange Community Primary School, Kettering, Northamptonshire

One Friday morning, as part of my second-year teaching practice, I was given an hour in which to 'do drama' with my class. This was quite scary as I had never actually taught drama before. However, I had been convinced of the educational benefits of drama by my English tutor (one Jo Boulton), and so had persuaded my class teacher to let me try out some of my new-found wisdom on the unsuspecting children of class 3.

In Monday's literacy lesson the children created story-boards for 'Jack and the Beanstalk' and wrote their own versions of the story. From this, I learned that the children knew the story well. I decided simply to take the suggested drama activities and work through them one after the other, using a version of the story from a book to fill in some of the details, as this seemed the most simple way to structure the lesson. As the children and I were inexperienced in drama, I made sure to talk to the children in detail about the aims of the drama session, so that they understood and were happy with what we were doing.

During the first activity the children *gradually* lost their inhibitions – only four children spoke the first time we said the line as a 'whole class'! However, by the time we were adding gestures to the line, class 3 were getting bolder, with some super suggestions coming directly from the children without any prompting on my part. For example, Andrew suggested that Jack's mum should have her arms crossed, her legs shoulder-width apart and her face screwed up into a scowl. He stood in the middle of the circle and demonstrated this to us all, setting off a succession of other suggestions and demonstrations from the rest of the class. As the activity progressed, even some of the quieter, more reluctant children began to offer suggestions. I was particularly pleased when Ronnie, a little boy who won't even sing in assembly, demonstrated the old lady's line in a slow, croaky voice, and with shoulders hunched.

The two activities which seemed to fire the children's imaginations the most were Activities 3 and 4, the advice alley and statementing. The advice alley worked beautifully (although my class insisted on standing in straight lines as they wanted to be able to see everybody – this made sense to me so I went with it!). The only example I gave was *'Perhaps the beans aren't really magic'*. They came up with such gems as *'They could be poisonous'*, *'I'm worried that they are dangerous'* and the classic *'Maybe they're bombs'*!

I was especially intrigued by the children's reactions to the statementing activity. The children were so keen to volunteer lines for Jack's mum that I gave every child two or three turns and afterwards they were still volunteering new ideas. Among their responses were *'I'm ashamed of you!'*, *'You're grounded!'* and *'Christmas is cancelled for you!'* It occurred to me that the children were drawing on personal experiences for this activity and this could be built on, perhaps in circle time or PSHE, as a way to discuss issues of conflict and punishment.

We worked through the activities up to and including Activity 5, which the children really enjoyed. I told them that they were to be 'film stuntmen' and to show me Jack climbing the beanstalk at the moment when he almost fell off. They loved it, and all wanted to show their sequence to the rest of the class.

After each activity I had been going back to the book to narrate the in-between stages of the story, so that the children were clear about where the activities fitted in. I also gave the class the opportunity to tell 'the story so far', to recap after each activity, before we started the next one.

The children groaned in unison when I told them to go and get ready for lunch at the end of the lesson, which indicated to me that they had enjoyed the lesson as much as I had. My teaching practice continues for another few weeks yet, and this lesson has really given me the confidence to teach lots more drama!

▌Roz Conlon's story
▌Preston Hedges Primary School, Northampton

I was a bit nervous at first. This was outside my usual experience. No aspects of the lesson bothered me. The only thing that was an issue was that I had to keep referring to the notes to make sure I was 'getting it right' – obviously that soon stopped! There were thirty Year 1 children who had not had much experience of drama.

After playing grandmother's footsteps as a warm-up I decided to start at the beginning and work my way through the plan numerically, using tasks or not according to how they were responding. I am used to having a pretty fluid lesson plan. I used the activity where children speak the mother's line at different volumes with different gestures and attitudes, and they responded really well. Some stumbled when speaking the line and making a gesture at the same time so this was good practice for them. When we brought two lines together with half the class saying one line and the other half saying the other, we got a good chorus going. Some found it difficult to keep to their own line. At this point there was good verbal and physical engagement and I felt this was a very successful coordination exercise. The children also seemed keen on persuading me to their point of view, i.e. to take the beans or sell the cow. . . I took the beans!

I then deviated from the plan here slightly, carrying on telling the story until the beans got thrown out of the window by the mother. I asked the whole group to stand in a circle, and took the role of Jack looking out of the window in the morning – *What did I see?* They could respond with anything they thought it might have grown into. This was essentially the advice alley, but I decided to have a circle, as I wanted to get moving and felt it might take too long to explain the alley to such a young group. There were lots of great responses – beans turned into four unicorns, plate of chips, large fish, castle and so on. Just at the point it felt right to move on, one participant said *'a beanstalk'* – which was very handy!

Still in circle, I asked whether we should climb it or cut it. They decided to climb, so all were involved in actions of climbing. Once we were at the top, I whispered that we should all spread right out, as *'Look, there's a giant asleep in the chair'*. We played the game keeper of the keys which the children loved, but they certainly didn't have much fear of this giant! There was lots of excitement – total involvement in the situation.

As soon as I, in role as the giant, had caught two girls, I asked the class to explain the situation and decide on the best course of action. Most of the responses involved painful punishments – throwing them down the beanstalk, tying them up, eating them, and drowning them. Finally, we agreed that perhaps it would be nice to let them go! So we all climbed back down the beanstalk and acted out giving the golden egg to the mother in different ways: nervous, excited, tired and so on. Then we all sat down to eat a feast.

Although the way in which the plan is structured allows for a non-linear focus on the story, as I had only one session with a group that I don't usually work with, I felt it made sense to work through the whole story and to reach a resolution. However, the class teacher mentioned that she would like to develop some of the ideas further, so the given structure was very useful for her. I also felt that the layout and instructions gave me, as a non-drama teacher, very clear examples of how to approach this type of work in a productive and engaging way.

Goodness – teaching drama is quite easy, isn't it!

▌Perry Hall's story
▌The Avenue Infants School, Wellingborough, Northamptonshire

I put aside an afternoon session for my Year 1 class to trial the 'Jack and the Beanstalk' drama. I read the sections through first, and decided to take it as it came and to try to cover as much as possible to aid continuity.

As a class, my children find it very difficult to concentrate for sustained periods and many have a 'yo-yo' approach to sitting on the floor. I therefore tried to keep the pace as upbeat as possible and to introduce movement around the room whenever I could. The children were very familiar with the story from previous literacy work and were keen to take part from the outset.

The first section, in which we changed the tone of our voices to emphasise different feelings, intrigued the children. I must admit that I hadn't approached this element in such a structured way with these children before. Some found it difficult to project their voices loud enough for others to hear effectively, while others had to work through a few furtive renditions of dalek and martian voices before they stopped 'entertaining' the others, and then they enjoyed the exercise for themselves. When they relaxed, I think that all the children were inspired by how many different ways they could give meaning to the same words. Gestures were carefully thought through and varied. I was pleased that the children found 'nagging' the most difficult to represent, as I sometimes feel that this is all they see from me during the day due to some challenging behaviour!

When approaching the next section, the children were quite happy to accept that Jack met an old lady in this version rather than an old man (as in ours) and, again, voice modulation and gestures were well thought through. I was pleased to see both girls and boys offering to stand up and perform. I noticed some good comic timing from various parties, although this might have been unintentional in one or two cases.

I wasn't sure how well the children would perform the chorus work but was pleasantly surprised. The children coped well with waiting for me, as Jack, to look at them so that they could speak. We had already done quite a lot of work in music on focusing on a conductor, and I think that this helped.

The advice alley proved to be more difficult for some of the children, as they got hooked on the fact that the beans would grow into a beanstalk and some found it hard to think of anything else. Nevertheless, we still had some interesting predictions from some of the children. These weren't necessarily those that shine in literacy sessions, which was good.

By the time we got around to Jack's mother's reactions the children were getting restless, so I sent them to tables with a piece of plain paper and a pencil each. I encouraged them to discuss with their friends what the disappointed mother would say and how she would stand as she said it. They were then asked to sketch Jack and his mother, showing her gesture, with a speech bubble coming from Jack's mum. The children were very keen to do this and worked quickly, showing that they had really thought about the scene. This made me think about the possibility of using 'story-boards', where children sketch gestures and expressions before some future drama work. I think that discussion and drawing made them more focused. On return from playtime, we resumed the activity and then acted it out with good vocal expressions and gestures.

Climbing up the beanstalk with appropriate facial grimacing was enjoyed, with much hilarity, by all. I was pleased that we attempted such exertions after playtime when everyone had already been to the toilet, as I think that it might have pushed a few 'over the edge' otherwise!

We had some excellent descriptive language when imagining the giant's room and filling in the blanks. This led to each child drawing a picture of how they visualised the room on the reverse of their speech bubble work (e.g. set design).

We had to leave the last section for another day but I feel that this will work well now that we have done the preparation work.

1 In the Jungle

The jungle is a happy place. All the animals live there together in harmony until one sad day. The lion, King of the jungle, calls them together to say that something is wrong. Can they find out the cause of the problem and solve it, or will they have to decide to leave their homes and make a journey to find a new home?

Time passes in the jungle. One day, the lion again decides to consult the animals about something that is worrying him. He has heard a strange sobbing sound coming from the river. Could it really be the scary crocodile making that terrible noise? Why is he in pain? Can the animals help him? Is anyone brave enough?

Aims

- To explore ideas about threats to society.
- To discuss feelings of jealousy towards a new sibling.
- To confront fears.
- To provide a challenge and present motives for asking questions.

Themes

- Sibling rivalry.
- Pollution.
- Dental hygiene.

Resources

Optional: Crown or cloak for the lion.

The imaginative play area can be designed as the jungle.

Notes

This selection of drama stories is based in a 'story-book jungle' with animals from different habitats living in the same environment. You may or may not want to be scientifically accurate about this.

It is important that you do not encourage the children to take on animal characteristics in this drama (e.g. growling, crawling on the ground). Encourage the children to 'be' the animals without behaving like them! They will be expected to be able to talk to you and to each other sensibly and you may have to set out these expectations explicitly at the start of the session.

The story about the crocodile is based on the story of *The Selfish Crocodile* by Charles Faustin.

In the jungle, by Charlie

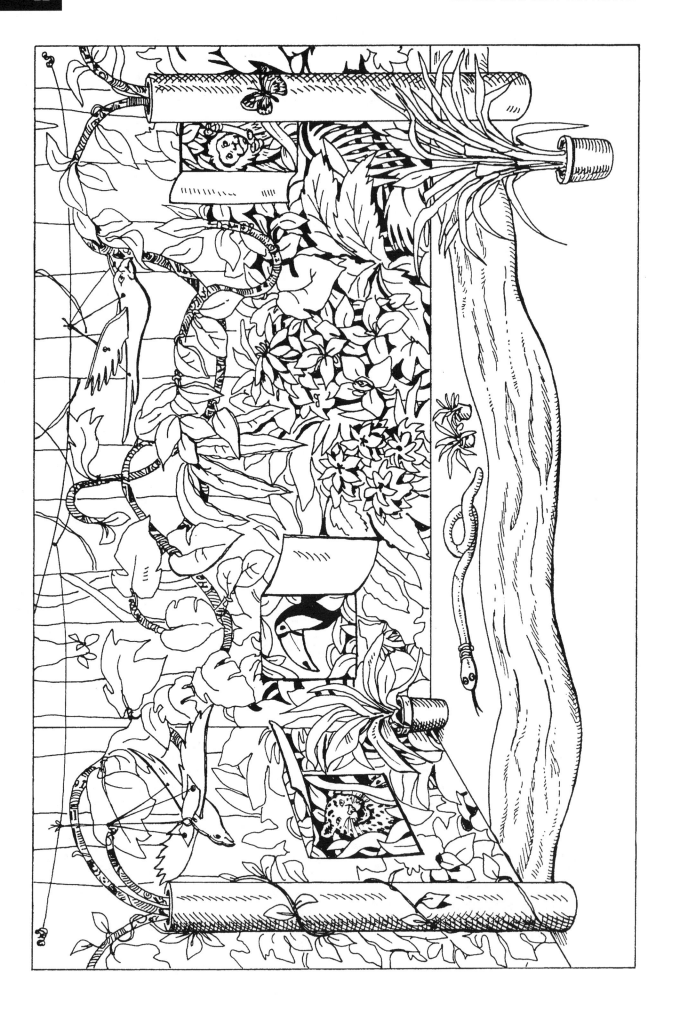

Activity 1   Who lives in the jungle?

Teacher's intentions

- To consider the animal life of a jungle.
- To build belief in their own roles and in the place.
- To practise being in an animal role without making exaggerated animal noises and exhibiting other overt animal behaviour.

Discussion: setting the scene

Ask the children to sit in a circle on the floor. Tell them that this represents the clearing in the jungle where the animals gather to have a chat and hold meetings when something important happens. Tell the children that you are going to be the lion, the King of the jungle in the story. You could use a crown and cloak to show when you are in role. Ask the children:

- *Which animal would you like to be in the jungle?*
- *Why do you think it would be fun to be a parrot?*
- *Please introduce yourselves to the group saying where you live in the jungle and what you like to eat.*

The children introduce themselves to the other 'animals'.

Dramatic play with teacher in role: the animals enjoy their environment

First narrate:

Once upon a time there was a peaceful jungle. All kinds of wonderful birds and animals lived happily together there. The big animals looked after the little animals and the little animals looked after the tiny ones. The lion was King of the jungle. His name was Leo. One lovely day in the jungle Leo was wandering around the jungle chatting to the animals and finding out what they were doing.

What would the animals be doing on a hot lazy day in the jungle?

Discuss possibilities and tell children to find a space where they will be in the jungle.

Tell the children that you will be the lion walking around the jungle.

In role as the lion, the teacher chats to the animals and asks them questions:

- *What have you been doing today?*
- *Have you seen the parrot this morning?*
- *I think I may go for a swim in the waterhole later if it stays hot.*
- *What can you see from here? Oh, you are lucky; you can see the river from your resting place here. What a lovely view!*

Discussion

What do we know about jungles (e.g. climate, vegetation)? What animals might we find living there? Make a list and add attributes (e.g. monkeys – swing from trees, eat fruit, carry babies).
What sounds and smells might we experience?

Stories

About the jungle: e.g. *Professor Noah's Spaceship* by Brian Wildsmith; *Walking Through the Jungle* by June Crebbin; *The Selfish Crocodile* by Charles Faustin; *The Enormous Crocodile* by Roald Dahl.

Collect...

Pictures or cuddly toys of jungle animals.

Art

Animal patterns. Children could consider what kinds of paw prints different animals would leave and use these in patterns.

Discussion in role: describing the scene

Ask the animals to sit together in the clearing by the river. As Leo, ask the animals to describe where they live in the jungle and talk about how they spend their time.

- *Hello monkeys, I saw you today. Tell us what you were doing.*
- *You hippos were in the waterhole, weren't you? What is it like wallowing around in all that mud?*

The elephant and the parrot, by Charlie

Activity 2   The King's new son

Teacher's intentions

- To use knowledge about the imaginary environment in a new situation.
- To encourage individuals to speak to the whole group.
- To consider tone of voice when asking questions.

Meeting: meet my new son!

As Leo, welcome the animals to the usual meeting place in the jungle. Tell them that your wife has just given birth to a cub. His name will be Yma. Pick up your imaginary cub and stroke him protectively. Ask the animals to come forward one at a time if they would like to stroke Yma. Ask them to tell Yma something that he will like to see or do in the jungle when he is older.

Hot seating: 'I'm jealous of the new cub'

Tell the children that you are going to be someone different in the next part of the story. You will be another lion cub, Yma's sister, who is not very happy. They will need to ask questions to find out what is wrong with her and try to cheer her up. Ask the children how they will approach someone who is sad. Try asking questions in different voices and aim for a calm, reassuring tone.

Yma's sister is called Gracie. She is jealous of the new cub Yma.

It isn't fair. I was the only cub until he arrived. Now everyone wants to see him and stroke him and no one is interested in me. Dad loves him more than he loves me.

Hopefully, the animals can give advice and reassurance to Gracie.

Geographical research

Use books or the internet to find out about jungle animals in their natural habitat. Use maps to locate rainforests.

Music and movement

Use music such as *The Carnival of the Animals* by Saint-Saëns. Physically explore how animals might move around in the jungle.

Poems and rhymes

This Little Puffin compiled by Elizabeth Matterson has a number of useful rhymes (e.g. 'Walking Through the Jungle', 'Let's See the Monkeys Climbing up a Tree', 'An Elephant Goes Like This Like That').

Activity 3   All is not well in the jungle

Map-making

Use a large sheet of paper and draw a simple map of the jungle, putting in the river, the monkeys' area, the trees where the parrots live and so on.

Teacher's intentions

● To use persuasive language.

● To encourage children to put forward a point of view.

● To encourage skills for making a case.

● To discuss wider issues of pollution and destruction of the natural environment.

Meeting with teacher in role: there is a problem in the jungle

Call the animals together and address them in role as Leo:

Animals of the jungle. Please come and sit with me in the clearing here by the river. There are some important things I need to discuss with you. I'm feeling very worried. It's been very noisy in the jungle recently. I've heard lots of rumbling sounds like big machines coming closer and closer. I have found that my drinking pool has been getting very dirty over the past few days and today it is full of rotting fruit. Have you seen anything unusual happening in your part of the jungle?

I would like you to go off in small groups or on your own and look around to spot if you can see or hear anything that is unusual. Look out for fallen trees or rotting fruit. You might see leaves falling off the trees or disturbed nests. Have a look around, then come back to tell me when I call you.

Collective drawing

Children draw an individual picture of something they would like to see in the jungle or a picture of themselves as the chosen animal. These may be stuck on to a large piece of paper to create a collective montage, or on to the map.

Dramatic play and meeting with teacher in role: identifying the problems

The children in role as the animals go off to look for unusual things and are called back to report on what they have found. Teacher in role as Leo addresses them again:

Thank you my friends for looking so carefully. Please tell me about anything you have seen or heard.

The animals tell the lion what they have seen. It would appear that something is threatening the jungle. The children may decide it is the human people or perhaps another animal threatening their peace and tranquillity.

Decide what should be done. Suggestions may include trying to follow the sounds (if any have been heard); setting a trap; writing a letter (if someone has been seen) or perhaps going together to confront the person or animal responsible.

Teacher in role and meeting: what can be done?

To resolve the drama you can take on the role of the person or animal causing problems in the jungle. There are a few possibilities that we have used:

1 You are a local person earning a living by cutting down trees. The jungle is being cut down because the wood is valuable. People in towns and other countries want furniture for their houses and you are just making a living. The machines used to cut the trees are polluting the water. Sorry, but you have to make money somehow to feed your family. The animals can try to persuade you to go somewhere else or stop and give reasons. The exchanges could include:

Animals:	*This is our home.*
Teacher in role:	*I'm sorry about that but I have a job to do. You could go somewhere else to live.*
Animals:	*We have nowhere to go.*
Teacher in role:	*Why don't you find another jungle?*
Animals:	*You're polluting our water.*
Teacher in role:	*I can't help it. Go somewhere else to get your water.*
Animals:	*It's not fair.*
Teacher in role:	*Well, I have to make money to feed my family. What about our families?*

The problem should be resolved (although not too easily). The animals may be able to persuade you to stop. Perhaps work practices are changed. Perhaps they decide to move to another jungle.

2 If it has been decided that it is an animal causing trouble you can take on this role, and the children in role as the other animals will find out why these things are happening.

The teacher in role might say:

I like it here and I want to stay. I heard it's a nice friendly place. I'm cutting down a few trees to make a clearing for me to live in. I don't like fruit so I'm throwing it into the river for fun. I like to bath in the waterhole as the water is clear and cool.

The animals try to use persuasion to stop it happening.

Still images
Create still images of animals in the jungle. Teacher taps each child on the shoulder and asks questions about what they are doing; what they can see, what they like to eat and so on.

Visit

Visit a zoo to find out more about different animals.

Activity 4   Meeting the crocodile

Teacher's intentions

- To focus on community spirit – working together to solve problems.
- To practise using persuasive language.
- To encourage discussion about ways of dealing with pain.
- To bring about discussion of fear of the dentist and maintaining personal hygiene.

Role on the wall: describing a crocodile

Talk about crocodiles. Ask children to give adjectives or phrases to describe crocodiles. Write down words as a list or around a large picture of a crocodile (from a book or an outline you have drawn).

Art

Make pictures or models of the animals.

Meeting with teacher in role: in the jungle lived a crocodile

Narrate the following, looking at individual children to invite them to fill in the gaps:

In the jungle lived a crocodile. All the other animals were... [look at one child and encourage them to give the next word in the story] *of the crocodile because he had such.... No one went near him. One day they heard a strange sound coming from the place where the crocodile lived. It sounded like sobbing. He sounded in pain.*

Teacher in role as the lion calls the animals to a meeting.

Has anyone heard the sobbing sound? What could be the matter? What should we do? The crocodile isn't very friendly to us so should we bother about him?

Hopefully the animals will want to find out what the problem is. Perhaps one or two brave animals could go and meet the crocodile.

Storytelling

Tell the end of the story or more stories about the characters.

Teacher in role: the crocodile is in pain

As the crocodile, you are grumpy and in pain. The children discover:

The problem is that I have toothache because I have broken my tooth on a stone.

I need help to pull out the tooth but I realise the animals are frightened of me.

What can be done?

I'm not paying to have my tooth pulled out and anyway I'm scared of dentists.

The children will probably want to help pull the tooth out. This is a job that needs careful planning.

- *What do they need to do?*
- *Will they all help?*
- *Who will climb into his mouth to tie the string to the tooth?*

Improvise pulling out the tooth – all stand in a long line and pull.

1, 2, 3, PULL!

The crocodile feels much better and thanks the animals for their help. He won't be so grumpy and frightening in the future. The animals may want to discuss why it is important to look after one's teeth, visit the dentist and brush teeth regularly.

Discussion: plenary

What happened in the different stories about the jungle? Retell the story, paying particular attention to the beginning, middle and end. How did the animals sort out the problems? What other adventures could the animals have?

Personal hygiene

What have we learned from the crocodile about keeping our teeth clean and having regular checks at the dentist?

• LINK TO •
'Farmer Roberts' Farm' and 'Helping at the Pet Shop' (Book 2) for animal stories

• LINK TO •
'Baz the Vandal' and 'The Dirty River' (Book 1) for caring for the environment stories

• LINK TO •
'The Health Centre' (Book 1) for health issues

2 Baby Bunting

Mr and Mrs Bunting are about to have a baby. They are very excited but are not really very sure about what they need to do to prepare for the new arrival. The children use all their knowledge and understanding about babies to help with the preparations. When the baby finally does arrive they are still asked to give advice to help keep the baby safe and well looked after.

Aims

- To share knowledge about caring for babies.
- To give help and advice to under-confident people.
- To consider gender stereotyping.

Themes

- Babies.
- Health and safety.

Resources

Optional: Apron/scarf/jacket, large doll, baby bath and towel, baby clothes.

Provided:

- Enlarged list of 'Things for Baby Bunting' (see Resource 1 below).
- Reminder cards (see Resource 2 below).

The imaginative play area can be designed as a baby nursery.

Notes

Although the main teacher role in this drama is written as female, it is equally possible for the role to be played as a male. Instead of the baby's mother being anxious about getting things right, the baby's father may also want to find out about what needs to be prepared for the arrival of the baby. She or he should not be played as 'simple' but as under-confident and needing help from the experts.

In this drama it is probably better to construct the imaginative play area as a follow-up activity, since it can reflect the ideas and opinions of the children as discussed in the drama.

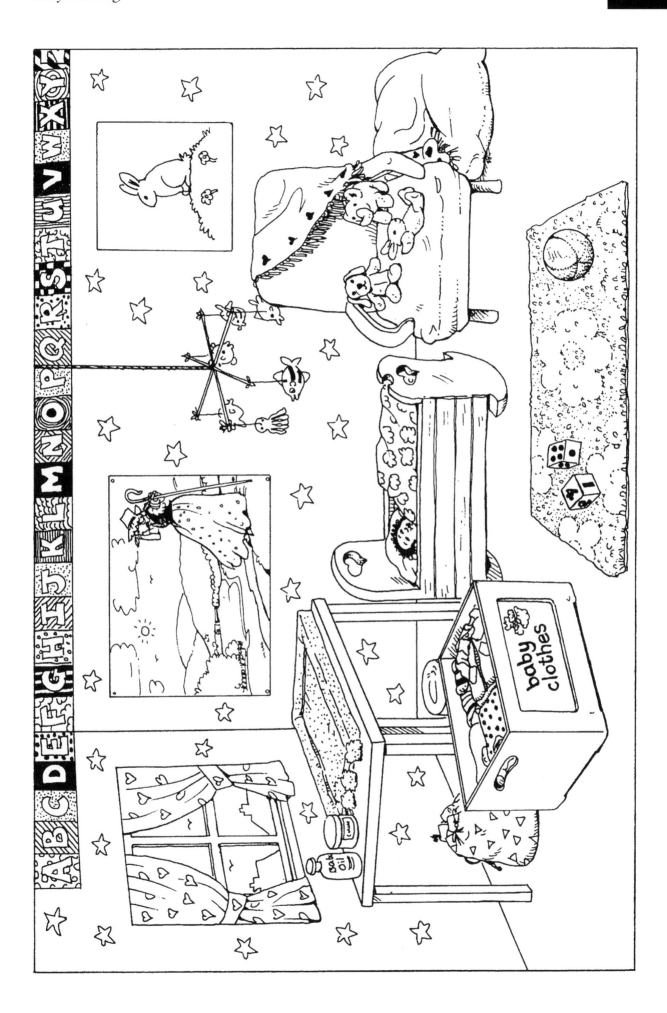

Things for Baby Bunting

Where will baby sleep?

What will baby eat?

What will baby wear?

What will baby say?

What toys will baby need?

What else should I think about?

Resource 2   Reminder cards

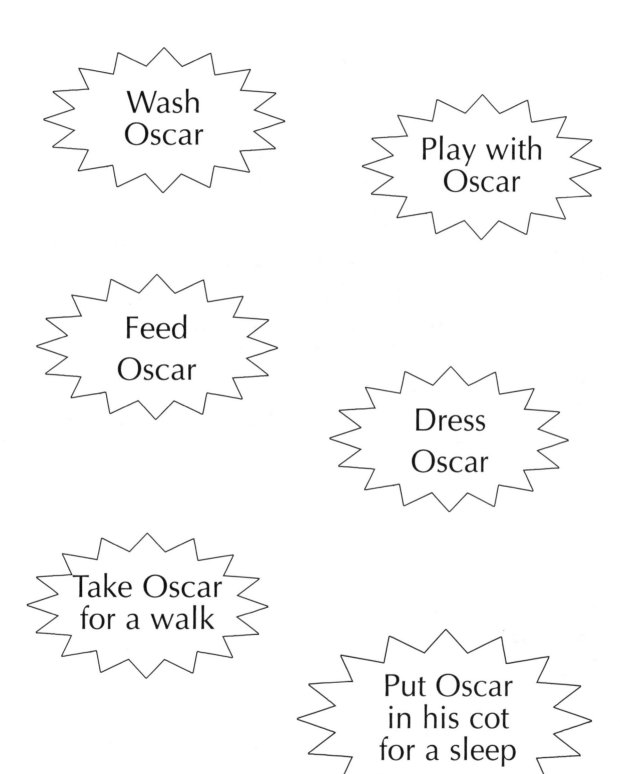

Feeding a baby

Discuss breast-feeding and look at examples of baby food.

Maths, PSHE and science activity

Collect pictures of people of different ages. Order the pictures showing growth from baby to adult. Discuss the process of growing up.

Matching baby photo game

Collect pictures of children and teachers as babies and try to identify who is who.

Activity 1   Mrs Bunting is having a baby

Teacher's intentions

- To share knowledge about babies.
- To give advice.

Discussion with teacher in role: meeting Mrs Bunting

Explain that the children will meet someone who is very nervous and who needs their help. Teacher speaks in role as Mrs Bunting:

Hello everyone. My name is Mrs Bunting but all my friends call me Katie. You see I am really excited because I'm having a baby quite soon and I need to start getting things organised. The thing is I don't know much about babies and I don't know many people to ask. I was wondering if you could help me because I bet you all know about babies and what they need.

Ask the children whether they have babies at home or know any babies. Tell them that you have started to make a list of the things you think are important. Show them the list and begin to ask questions about items on it. Use pictures from catalogues for children to choose from (e.g. A cot or a double bed?).

- *Will the baby need a big bed, do you think?*
- *Will the baby like fish fingers for tea?*
- *Will the baby wear clothes like yours?*
- *How will I know if the baby wants anything?*

Stick pictures to the list after listening to the children's advice. Write notes to remind Katie what she needs to remember, e.g. Babies drink milk. Buy some nappies!).

Activity 2   Decorating the nursery

Teacher's intentions

- To discuss colour stereotypes.
- To build belief in the nursery.

Discussion with teacher in role: making decisions

Tell the children that Mrs Bunting is still getting ready for the baby and needs their help again.

Hello again. I'm really pleased to see you today because I'm just about to start decorating the nursery and I can't decide what to do. I've got some tins of paint here. Could you help me decide which colour will be best? This paint is bright pink. What do you think? Or how about this lovely blue?

Discuss appropriateness of colours and the traditional view of genders and colour. Come to an agreement or perhaps choose some wallpaper with teddies on instead! Discuss and make choices about furniture for the nursery.

Collect
Make a class collection of favourite dolls and teddies. These can be looked after and used for demonstrating how to bath or dress a baby.

Dramatic play: decorating the nursery

Children help Katie to decorate the nursery. She helps where she can and suggests things which are not always a good idea.

Let's start by mixing up the paste/paint. Has everyone got a brush? Be careful now; don't slop it all over the place! Can you paint the window frame? How about the door? Will we need new curtains, do you think? Could you make some for me? There are some nails sticking out here. It won't matter, will it?

Thank you so much. You've worked really hard. Let's have a look around the room.

Can you help me to move this cupboard in?

Ask children to describe what they can see in the room now it has been decorated.

- *The wallpaper has teddies on it.*
- *The paint is yellow.*
- *The floor has a new carpet.*
- *There's a light with a shade.*

Access nursery rhymes websites
http://www.geocities.com/ elayne_au/LITTLEBOYBLUE.html. http://www.geocities.com/ singingkid1/BabyBunting.html.

Discussion in role: children advise

Ask the children to sit in a square shape (to represent the walls of the nursery).

There's just one more special piece of furniture to put into this lovely room – the cot. Isn't it beautiful? Can you describe it? What is it made from? What colour is the blanket? Where shall we put it in the room? Should it be near the window or in the middle of the room?

Thank you so much. The room is now ready for the baby. I hope it arrives soon. I'm not sure about names. Have you any suggestions if it is a girl? What about boys' names?

Make a list of names.

Nursery rhymes

Read nursery rhymes, particularly lullabies. Many useful rhymes may be found in *This Little Puffin* by Elizabeth Matterson. These can include 'Bye Baby Bunting', 'Hush-a-bye, Baby', 'Little Boy Blue'.

Bye Baby Bunting
Bye Baby Bunting,
Daddy's gone a-hunting
To get a little rabbit-skin
To wrap my Baby Bunting in.

Hush-a-bye, Baby
Hush-a-bye, baby, on the tree-top
When the wind blows the cradle will rock.
When the bough breaks the cradle will fall
And down will come baby, cradle and all.

Little Boy Blue
Little Boy Blue come blow your horn, the sheep's in the meadow, the cow's in the corn;
But where is the boy who looks after the sheep?
He's under a haystack fast asleep.
Will you wake him? No, not I, for if I do,
he's sure to cry.

Activity 3   Meeting the new baby

Teacher's intentions

- To encourage decision-making.
- To encourage individual contributions.

Discussion and dramatic play: a present for the baby

Tell the children that Katie has had her baby and it is a boy called Oscar. They have been invited round to meet Oscar this afternoon and wouldn't it be nice to take him a present? Discuss what present they would like to take. Draw the present on a piece of paper or practise picking up the imaginary present, wrapping it in paper and writing a card.

Ritual: giving the presents to Oscar

Children sit in a circle. Teacher in role as Katie greets them, carrying the new baby, who is asleep wrapped up in a shawl.

Hello everyone. Oscar is asleep at the moment. You've brought him some presents! How lovely. Would you like to come up one at a time and give them to him? You can put them down here and open them for him if you like. Would you like to come first and tell me what you've brought? A rattle, how lovely! A baby-grow. He needs some of those!

Baby Bunting and his elephant, by Charlie

Dressing a baby
Learn how to put on a baby's nappy.
Choose suitable clothes.

Shared writing of a poem
When I was a baby I could...
Now I'm a child I can...
When I am older I will...

Music
Use instruments to create soothing music to lull baby to sleep.

PSHE discussion
Talk about ways of keeping safe and healthy.

Art and literacy
Make a poster showing how to take care of a baby.

Collect baby vocabulary
e.g. nappy, cot/crib/cradle/Moses basket, bib, dummy/soother, buggy, pram, steriliser, formula milk.

Activity 4 Keeping the baby safe and well

Teacher's intentions

● To highlight health and safety issues.
● To encourage children to give advice.

Discussion and dramatic play: checking what to do

Children sit in a circle and teacher speaks in role as Katie:

Hello everyone. It's lovely to see you again. I wonder if you could help me. Today is the first day that I'm on my own looking after Oscar. The midwife isn't coming to help me any more and I'm a bit nervous. She's left some reminder cards of things I need to do and I put them in the right order. But something awful happened – I dropped the cards! Now I don't know what order to do things in. Shall we have a look?

Katie shows the children separate reminder cards and they try to decide on the best order for doing the tasks (see Resource 2). For example:

● Feed Oscar.
● Wash Oscar.
● Dress Oscar.
● Take Oscar for a walk.
● Play with Oscar.
● Put Oscar in his cot for a sleep.

The children may suggest other things to add to the list (e.g. cuddle, singing).

Ask the children to show you how to do the jobs on the list by using dolls and teddies to bath and feed if there are enough available for one each or one between two. Alternatively, the jobs can be mimed using imaginary babies. Katie may need to be helped a lot by the children as she is still not sure how to hold Oscar properly, what he will eat and so on. She even suggests they hang the cot up in a tree in the garden for it to swing, as in the rhyme 'Hush-a-bye, Baby'. The children should persuade her that this is not a good idea!

Discussion: plenary

What do we know about looking after babies? What are the most important things we need to remember to keep a baby healthy and safe?

• LINK TO •
'In the Jungle' (Book 2) for stories about new babies and sibling rivalry

• LINK TO •
'The Health Centre' (Book 1) for health issues

• LINK TO •
'The Teddy Bears' Picnic' (Book 1) for stories about caring

3 Pirate Adventure

The children are a new crew on a pirate ship. They learn the jobs on board and then discover that the captain is against fighting. After surviving a storm, they reach the island where the treasure is buried. They follow the map through woods and over streams until they reach the spot marked on the map. There they discover that someone else has got to the treasure first. They must now try to negotiate a share of the treasure without upsetting their captain by fighting.

Aims

- To consider the rights and wrongs of violent behaviour.
- To invite critical thinking about expectations of people.
- To develop an understanding of how to create atmosphere by using sounds and words.

Themes

- Pirates.
- Greed.
- Ownership.
- Exploration.
- Good and bad/right and wrong.
- Stealing.

Resources

Optional:

- Pirate story-books.
- Pictures of pirates.
- Items of pirate costume.
- Large sheets of paper.
- Crayons or felt-tip pens.
- Enlarged version of treasure map (see page 30).

The imaginative play area can be designed as a pirate ship or a treasure island.

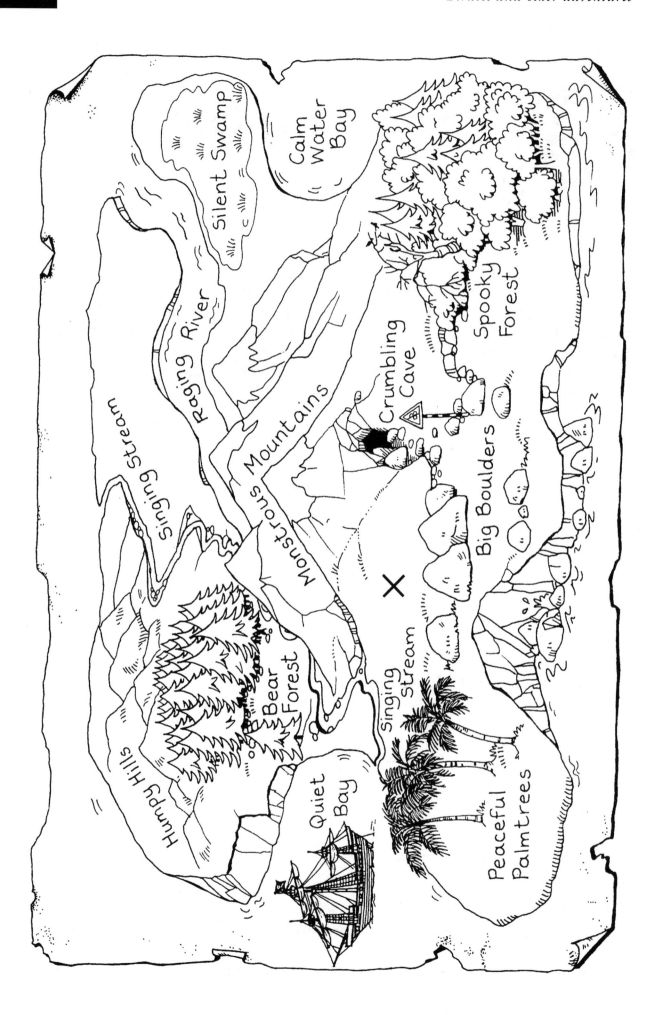

Activity 1   Life on board ship

Teacher's intentions

- To develop children's roles.
- To introduce the teacher's role.
- Setting the scene.

Teacher in role and mime: welcome to my ship!

Teacher in role as captain of the ship welcomes everyone aboard:

I know that some of you have never been to sea on a ship before but I'm pleased to see that you're happy and excited to be here. I hope you don't think it's an easy life on board ship. There's plenty of work to be done and you'll soon learn all the jobs.

Are there any questions?

Now there will be lots to do on board. Do you know what kind of jobs you will need to do?

Take suggestions from the children. Introduce your crew to one job at a time (e.g. scrubbing the decks, climbing the rigging, polishing the railings, rolling barrels). Mime each activity all together and then ask the children to choose which will be their special chosen job.

Improvisation: working on the ship

Children do their special jobs. The captain walks around, chatting and checking on the work:

- *The water in your bucket looks a bit dirty.*
- *How did you get that rail so shiny?*
- *What are you doing?*
- *Is that heavy?*
- *How many ships have you been on?*
- *What are you looking forward to doing when we set sail?*

Game
'Captain's Coming' (see 'Games', p. 98).

Read stories
Pirates or other seafarers (e.g. *The Man whose Mother was a Pirate* by Margaret Mahy).

Brainstorm
What do we know about pirates?

Costumes or props...
Associated with pirates (e.g. eye patch and toy parrot displayed). Discuss who might have an eye patch and why.

Storytelling

Begin with a pirate ship setting off in search of adventure and plunder.

Draw

Draw individual pictures of children dressed as pirates. A Rogues Gallery can be presented.

Codes

Make up simple codes with flags or hand signals (e.g. wave right hand means hello, wave both hands means goodbye).
Make up a coded message to put in a bottle where letters are substituted by pictures:

a = 🙂

b = ⭐

c = ⊗

Activity 2   The peaceful pirate captain

Teacher's intentions

- To introduce a dilemma.
- To use persuasion and reassurance.
- To look at different viewpoints.

Whole group improvisation: the captain is worried

The captain has gone very quiet. He spends a lot of time sitting on his own. What could be wrong with him? Children discuss possibilities.

The crew decide to find out what is wrong with him. The teacher in role as captain sits in a chair with the crew sitting around on the floor:

Hello everyone. It's good to see you all. Are you getting on with your work OK? Are you enjoying the trip? [Big sigh]

Look worried, frown, wring hands until children ask what is wrong. The captain gradually gives the following information:

- *I don't think I'm a very good pirate captain . . .*
- *I'm not like the other pirate captains I meet . . .*
- *I'll let you down . . .*
- *You'll be disappointed with me when you know the truth . . .*
- *I don't want us to meet another pirate ship . . .*
- *I'm scared . . .*
- *I don't want to hurt anybody – I don't like fighting . . .*
- *I love following maps and digging for treasure . . .*
- *But, what do we do if we want something and someone else has it?*

The intention is to bring the children around to accepting the unexpected viewpoint of the pirate captain and to plan alternative methods of negotiation. Solutions to the problem are various; for example:

- Crew suggest they become treasure hunters instead.
- All agree on how to plunder without hurting anyone.

Activity 3 A stormy night

Teacher's intentions

- To develop listening skills.
- To respond physically to narration.
- To use music and sound to create storm effects.

Narration and mime: the storm

The children listen and join in by miming in silence to what the teacher describes:

The crew were all asleep in their hammocks when the wind began to blow. The hammocks began to swing from side to side. The crew slowly awoke, stretching their arms and looking around them. They heard the rain pattering on the deck. They heard the captain calling them. Up they jumped and got dressed as quickly as they could. They climbed up the ladder to the deck. By now the rain was banging against the sails. The sails had to be tightened so they climbed up the mast and pulled hard on the ropes. Back down on deck the sea was rocking the ship so hard that the crew were thrown to one side [point to the left] *and then the other* [point to the right]. *When the storm was over they returned to their hammocks exhausted.*

Pirate pictures
How many different pirates can you draw?

Making sound effects: the storm

The teacher conducts the children as they create the storm using handclaps and vocal noises only. This will need to be practised. Begin by gentle blowing for wind sounds and finger tapping for light rain. The storm builds up gradually with increasing volume, cracks of thunder and strong handclaps, and then decreases until there is a silent calm.

Songs and rhymes
Sea-shanties (e.g. 'What Shall We Do with the Drunken Sailor?'). *This Little Puffin* by Elizabeth Matterson contains a number of good rhymes including 'The Big Ship Sails through the Alley, Alley O' and 'This is the Boat, the Golden Boat that Sails on the Silver Sea'.

Drawings

Children draw pictures of an ending, or different parts of the story for a class storyboard.

Collective drawing

Children may want to create a large map as a collective drawing as an alternative to the one provided. Collective drawings of the pirate captain or the pirate ship could also be drawn.

Story circle

Children create their own ending to the story or further stories about the pirates.

Make

Make treasure out of brightly coloured sweet papers and buttons, and treasure chests out of cardboard.

Activity 4   Treasure challenge

Teacher's intentions

- To present a challenge.
- To encourage children to use persuasive language.

Narration and mimed action with teacher in role: looking at the map

After sailing for three days, the crew spot the island on their treasure map. They anchor the ship in the bay and wade on to the beach. The captain clutches the map excitedly.

The captain spreads out the map and invites crew to identify the route from the bay to the treasure marked by an X (see map on page 30).

The captain leads the crew over the hill and through the wood where bears and other dangerous animals may lurk. The teacher talks about the imaginary journey in order to bring it to life, encouraging the children to climb over imaginary boulders and crawl under imaginary vines (e.g. *'Keep your eyes open for snakes!' 'How will we get over this river?'*)

No props are required, only imagination. Eventually, teacher narrates:

The pirates find the spot and are horrified to find a big hole. Standing next to the hole is another pirate.

Teacher in role: *This is my treasure!*

The teacher takes the role of the new pirate. The distinction can be made clearer by wearing a different item of clothing and assuming a very different attitude.

So, you thought you'd find some treasure, did you? Well, I got here first. It's all loaded in my ship. So there's nothing you can do about it.

The children may respond in a variety of different ways. For example:

- Threaten to fight. The teacher should say she knows that they have promised their captain not to fight and that they will get into trouble with him if they do.
- Negotiate and resolve, which may give them some treasure. The teacher may need to encourage this by saying, *'Why should I share it with you?'* and the children can then explain that they are nice pirates, or that they need the money.

Discussion: plenary

Discuss the story and the different pirate adventures. Depending on the decision they made, discuss whether it was fair to share or not to share the treasure? Where might the treasure have come from in the first place?

Make
Make 'authentic' treasure maps using tea-stained paper and charcoal sticks.

• **LINK TO** •

'The Lost Hat', 'Goldilocks', 'Baz the Vandal' (Book 1), 'Jack and the Beanstalk', 'Under the Sea' (Book 2) and 'Finders Keepers' (Book 3) for moral issues

• **LINK TO** •

'Mary Mary and the Giant' (Book 2) for anti-stereotypes

• **LINK TO** •

'Under the Sea' (Book 2) for sea stories

The pirate ship, by Charlie

© Jo Boulton and Judith Ackroyd (2004) *Pirates and other adventures*, David Fulton Publishers.

Jack and the Beanstalk

When Jack's mother finds they have no money left for food, she has no choice but to ask Jack to sell their cow. He must get as much as he can for it because they desperately need the money. Jack faces a dilemma when he is offered magic beans rather than money for the cow. Perhaps the beans will bring good luck. But he knows how desperate his mother is for money for food this very day. He decides to take the beans. When the beanstalk grows, Jack climbs up to see the giant sleeping beside a pile of golden eggs. His attempt to creep up and retrieve the eggs fails when the giant wakes and booms that the boy is a wicked thief. He asks the children what he should do with Jack. How should the giant punish him for trying to steal?

Aims

- To develop children's understanding of the importance of tone and expression for communicating meaning.
- To encourage creativity in making up story endings.
- To invite group shared responsibility.

Themes

- Exploring fairytales.
- Demonstrating emotions.
- Stealing – moral dilemmas.

Resources

Optional:

- A few beans, such as broad beans or jellybeans.
- Props to represent golden eggs or gold coins.
- Real beans/bulbs/seeds or avocado pear stones for planting.

The imaginative play area can be designed as a giant's house with oversized objects. Alternatively it could be a castle or Jack's cottage.

Notes

In this drama the children explore nuances of language in a very simple way. They say lines in different ways and with different gestures so that the meanings change. It can easily be related to everyday class speech in which gesture, tone and facial expression are often more significant to meaning than the words. 'I didn't do it', for example, can be said with many different overtones! This work takes the power from the phrase, *'I only said...'* since the response is inevitably, but *how* did you say it?

Jack and the Beanstalk, by Charlie

Activity 1   The cow must be sold

Teacher's intentions

- To introduce the story.
- To consider the way we understand language through more than the words.
- To experiment ways of changing meaning with tone of voice and gesture.

Narration: setting the scene

The familiar story is told up to the moment when Jack is sent on his way to sell the cow. They are desperate for money for food. The last thing that Jack's mother says to him is, *'Get lots of money for food, Jack!'*

Whole group line delivery: what is Jack's mother's concern?

How might she have said these words to show she is desperate?

Make a hand gesture to indicate when to say the line all together. Try the line at different volumes by moving your arm up for loud and down for soft.

What gesture may she have used?

All try pointing a finger with the line.

What do we understand by this? (Giving clear instruction to Jack.)

All try holding up hands against her head. (She is desperate for Jack to get this right.)

Try these lines loudly and softly and see what difference it makes.

Some children may wish to deliver the line with a gesture of their own. They are encouraged to see how the same lines can communicate different meanings. How about:

- *As if she is weak with hunger? And the gestures?*
- *As if she is a very strong and powerful woman?*
- *As if she is always nagging Jack?*

Narration or narration and action: Jack meets the old lady

You can either narrate this to the children while they are seated, or invite them to stand up and imagine they are Jack walking, getting tired and holding out his hand.

Jack walks towards market with the cow. He is getting tired when he meets a strange old woman. She offers him magic beans instead of money for the cow. He explains that he needs money, but she says,

'Take these magic beans, my boy.'

Whole group line delivery: the old lady's words

- *How might she have said these words to show she is desperate? What gesture may she have used?*
- *What if she wanted Jack to know that the beans were magic?*
- *What if she meant to frighten Jack into taking the beans?*
- *What if she wanted to be very kind to Jack?*

Again, the class can chant the lines together in different ways with different gestures.

Story-books
Read different versions of the well-known 'Jack and the Beanstalk' fairytale.

Grandmother's Footsteps (see 'Games', p. 97)
This game develops physical coordination. Here it prepares children for the quick reactions required in the chorus work of Activity 2 when the teacher in role as Jack looks to his mother and the old lady.

Websites

There are many websites with 'Jack and the Beanstalk' stories. A good animated story may be found at http://www.bbc.co.uk/cbeebies/stories/jack_s.shtml.

Read other 'Jack' stories

Jim and the Beanstalk by Raymond Briggs. Jim visits the son of Jack's giant in a wonderful sequel.
Jack and the Three Sillies by Richard Chase. A humorous American version of a 'Jack' story from England.

Activity 2   Jack's decision to take the beans

Teacher's intentions

- To develop vocal control and a sense of timing.
- To practise concentration when responding to a cue.
- To consider choices.

Chorus work: Jack's choice

Divide the class into two halves with each half at either end of the room. One half represents Jack's mother and says her line (*'Get lots of money for food, Jack'*) and the other, the old lady (*'Take these magic beans, my boy'*). Agree with each side how they want to say their line, making a choice from the earlier delivery experiments (e.g. mother desperate and old woman sounding scary).

Teacher in role as Jack stands in the middle of the room holding the beans in his hands. He is wondering what to do. When he looks towards the old lady, the children must all repeat her line over until the moment he turns away. Then they fall silent as quickly as they did in 'Grandmother's Footsteps'. When Jack looks at his mother's group, they repeat her line until he looks away again.

Jack will look down at some point, so the children will all be silent then. He may toy with the beans and may add some words in between, such as:

- *Perhaps something good will come of the beans.*
- *My mother is so hungry. I shouldn't do this.*

This activity is about coordination, and the concentration to respond at the appropriate time. It is fun to do, and it highlights Jack's dilemma. Finally, he makes the decision:

'Have our cow. I will take your beans!'

Activity 3   The beans could be magic

Teacher's intentions

- To provide an opportunity for a contribution from each child in a safe context.
- To stretch the imagination in search of different possibilities.

Advice alley: are the beans really magic?

The children form two winding lines facing each other to create the path Jack followed on his way home. The teacher or a child holds the beans and very slowly wanders down the path (e.g. between the two lines of children). As Jack passes each child, they say how they think the beans might be magic or what they might grow into.

- *They may turn into gold.*
- *They could grow into a beanstalk.*
- *They will make him rich.*
- *They aren't magic at all.*

> **Beans, bulbs and seeds**
> A range of these could be examined and guesses made about what they will grow into before they are planted. Drawings are made of them before they are planted. They will be observed as they grow and plants identified.

Activity 4   Jack's mother's reaction

Teacher's intentions

- To consider different types of responses.
- To practise earlier learning of gesture and tone to communicate meaning.
- To use very little or no speech.

Statementing: what might Jack's mother say?

What might Jack's mother have said when Jack came home with the beans?

Children make a few suggestions and share ideas of gestures that might help to make the meaning clear.

Was she angry? Upset? Desperate? Crazy?

Stand in the middle of a circle of children. The teacher will approach anyone in rule as Jack holding out the beans. The child gives a response that his mother might give. Jack can react and then move on to another child in the circle. Another line for the mother is heard, and Jack may or may not respond before moving on to another, until each child has had a turn to give a line. These might include:

- *Go to your bed at once!*
- *What will we do for food now?*
- *How can you be so stupid?*

> **Story recordings**
> Listening to stories recorded by actors provides further examples of the way language is used differently. How different are giants' voices? Which do we find most frightening? What makes them sound frightening, since it is only a voice? There are no visual aids to meaning.

Beanstalk sculpture

An ongoing project to make part of the beanstalk appear to come out of the floor and wind up through the ceiling. Twisted rolls of paper may be woven into each other, gradually making it thicker and stronger. It could also be a papier mâché project!

Activity 5   Climbing the beanstalk

Teacher's intentions

- To move the story on.
- To use physical activity to tell the story.

Narration: Jack's discovery

The next part of the story is told in as much detail as you wish. Jack sleeps well and perhaps his mother sleeps not so well! In the morning Jack sees the huge beanstalk. When he looks up he realises it goes up and up as far as he can see. He decides to climb it.

Narration with mimed action: climbing high

Invite the children to climb the beanstalk as Jack. Lead the children in action through describing climbing the beanstalk and demonstrating the gestures.

If you want to use this to teach left and right sides, don't forget to turn your body away, though you may want to keep your head turned towards the children. If left and right is not important for you, face the children to show your facial expressions, concentrating on what you are doing.

He first put his right hand up to the highest branch he could reach. Then he pulled himself up by placing his left foot on a lower branch. Slowly he raised his right foot, but...he slipped and nearly fell. Luckily his right hand was strong enough to hang on.

Keeper of the Keys (see 'Games', p. 97)

This game encourages physical control and dexterity. Here it is a way of working towards the dramatic moment when Jack tries to steal from the giant in Activity 6.

Activity 6   Stealing up on the giant

Teacher's intentions

- To provide the opportunity to develop physical agility and control.
- To practise communication skills.
- To consider the consequences of Jack's actions.
- To introduce ethical questions about distribution of wealth.

Narration: creeping into the giant's house

The children are invited to fill the gaps in this narration so that together they will build up a picture of the giant's room.

When Jack eventually reached the top of the beanstalk he found himself in a huge room, with huge furniture and huge walls, doors and ceilings. He saw a huge...and a massive.... He saw the most enormous...and a gigantic....

Under the chair that was as big as a..., Jack saw some golden eggs. The giant was sound asleep, so Jack wondered if he could creep over and reach under the giant's chair and get hold of some of those eggs. If he got even one egg, he and his mother would never be hungry again.

Whole class improvisation/game and discussion: the end of the story

Take the role of the giant and sit in a chair snoring. The children sit in a large circle around you and play the action as in the game 'Keeper of the Keys' (see 'Games'). They try to creep slowly nearer to the chair with the aim to get the eggs. However, every time they get somewhere near, the giant moves, grunts or twitches, which sends them back to the edge where they can't be seen. This also echoes the game 'Grandmother's Footsteps' (see 'Games', p. 97).

When a child reaches out to get the eggs, the giant touches him – *Got you!* – then jumps up on to a chair and says in a big, deep voice:

This boy is a thief! This boy has entered my house when he wasn't invited. He didn't even ask to come in or knock on the door! He has crept up on me in my sleep and tried to steal my eggs.

I am a strong giant, but I am a fair giant. What do you think I should do with him? Shall I eat him? Shall I crush him? Should he be made to clean my house each day for five years?

Tell me, how should I punish this boy?

The children will probably explain that Jack and his mother are hungry and that he didn't mean any harm. The drama ends once the children have decided what should happen. Many want the giant and Jack to be friends and for the giant to let Jack have just one egg. The giant may insist on an apology. The giant may decide it is wrong for him to have so much and not even use it, when others like Jack's family are starving. It may turn out that the giant had worked for his wealth, or had stolen it himself. Perhaps, long ago, he had plundered the village at the foot of the beanstalk!

Whatever the children decide can be discussed and acted out.

Discussion: plenary

Discussion about who was right and who was wrong in this story.

Consider lines we might use in everyday life and consider the different ways they could be said and which ways are more appropriate in different contexts. An example is:

All right. You can borrow my ruler.

Try saying it:

- With affection.
- To tease.
- As if you don't want to lend it.
- To upset the borrower.

Sizes
Make a little book of little things and a large book of large things.

Music
Use musical instruments to make contrasting soft, creeping music for Jack and loud, roaring music for the giant.

• LINK TO •
'Goldilocks' (Book 1), 'Cinderella' (Book 2) and 'Billy Goats Gruff' (Book 3) for traditional tales

• LINK TO •
'Mary Mary and the Giant' (Book 2) for giant stories

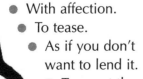
• LINK TO •
'The Lost Hat', 'Goldilocks' and 'Baz the Vandal' (Book 1), 'Under the Sea' (Book 2) and 'Finders Keepers' (Book 3) for moral issues

© Jo Boulton and Judith Ackroyd (2004) *Pirates and other adventures*, David Fulton Publishers.

CHAPTER 5

Helping at the Pet Shop

The pet shop is a busy place. Ms Lanteri at the pet shop welcomes the children who have come to work at Pets R Us. The children are all eager to learn and help with the animals. They learn how to look after different animals and to advise people who are buying new pets. To help one customer they create a fish tank with all its different parts.

Aims

- To share and use knowledge of animals and pets.
- To understand why people have pets.
- To know how to keep animals fit, healthy and safe.
- To give advice about pets.

Themes

- Caring for animals.
- Responsibility.
- Health and safety.

Resources

Optional:

- Toy animals.
- Bandages.
- Large cardboard boxes for cages.

The imaginative play area can be designed as a pet shop.

Notes

Creating the fish tank in Activity 4 may be done within the classroom or in the hall, depending on the number of children in your group. If you are working with a small group you may like to use PE equipment (such as benches) to create the tank and the children become the filter, heater and fish. It is a good idea to decide 'parts' in your own mind before you begin the activity. It is useful to have a picture of a fish tank for the children to look at. Once the tank is created the children love to bring it to life.

Activity 1   Pet shop game

Teacher's intentions

- To provide a fun introduction to the drama.

Game: different pets

This game is played like 'Fruit Bowl' (see 'Games', p. 98), except with the names of pets rather than fruit. The children sit on chairs in a circle. Each is allocated one of three names (e.g. rabbits, fish or lizards). A caller in the middle of the circle calls out one of the names (e.g. rabbits), and all the rabbits have to leave their seats and find another chair to sit on. The caller's aim is to sit on a chair too. Whoever is left without a chair is the caller in the middle. If 'pet shop' is called, everyone has to leave their chairs and find another one.

Activity 2   Meeting the helpers

Teacher's intentions

- To build belief in the roles of the children and the teacher.
- To use appropriate formal language.
- To learn the basics about handling pets.

Meeting: the helpers are welcomed

Tell the children you are going to be the manager at a large pet shop called Pets R Us. The children will be young people who have come to work in the shop.

Good morning everyone. My name is Ms Lanteri. Welcome to Pets R Us. It's lovely to see you all. I know you are here to learn about the job of working in a pet shop. Can you introduce yourselves to me so I know who you are? I like to know all the trainees who are going to be here working with me.

Trainees introduce themselves individually. Shake hands and welcome each to the shop.

Excellent. Now, I wonder if you know the kind of things that you need to learn about?

Take a few suggestions from the trainees.

Good. Now before we start to look at any of the animals that we have here today, what do you think is the first thing I want you all to do?

Wash your hands! Put on an overall! That's right. We need to make sure we are clean before we touch the animals because there are some very young animals that might catch germs, and some of the animals might be unwell.

Give out imaginary overalls and show the trainees where to wash their hands.

Mimed activity: handling the animals

Now, I'd like you all to practise handling a pet. The animals need to be held differently. We have lots of rabbits in cages over here. They all have their names written on the cages. Watch to see how I hold it.

Mime opening the cage and picking up the rabbit. Describe what you are doing.

Open the cage gently so you don't scare the rabbit. See how gentle I am because rabbits can be easily scared. Give it a stroke and a tickle under the chin, like this. It is possible to lift rabbits by their ears, but this always strikes me as rather harsh, so please don't do it here. Now it's your turn. Pick up a rabbit from one of these cages. Check what its name is. Show your rabbit to your friend and introduce your rabbit.

After a while, suggest that the rabbits are all put into a run to have some exercise.

Hamsters can be handled similarly. Here point out that they have no tails, but the males have stumps. Mime how to move your hands in front of each other so the hamster can walk on the spot in your open palms.

Choose other animals. Each time, model how they are caught and handled and then invite the children to lift one too. Snakes are held behind their heads so that you can control its head. Movement is thus restricted.

Matching…
Pictures of pet food appropriate to each pet.

Guess the animal
Descriptions of different animals to read out and guess. For example:
● This animal is small and fluffy. It hops around the garden and has long ears.
● This animal is large. Its coat is smooth. It is white with black spots. It barks.

Activity 3   A customer needs advice

Teacher's intentions

● To encourage talk.

● To develop understanding of the needs of pets and their owners' responsibilities.

● To reflect on the care required for different animals.

● To consider which pets are suitable for different people.

Meeting in role: a customer arrives

Teacher takes the role of a customer, Rani, who asks if she can speak with them about a pet.

I so want a pet. It would be lovely to have something to cuddle, or to play with, or to take out. I am wondering what sort of pet would be best for me.

● *Which pets could I cuddle/play with/take out/ride?*

● *What pets do you have yourselves?*

● *What do I need to do or have, to look after these different pets?*

Dramatic play: looking after the pets

Rani asks:

● *Could you show me how to take care of the pets?*

● *What would I need to do to look after a pony?*

● *How do I take care of a dog?*

● *Do I need any special equipment to keep a snake?*

After some general discussion, tell the children to choose in pairs which pet they will be talking about. They should imagine their stable, cage or tank and start doing what needs to be done. They can be mixing feed, cleaning out the hutch, brushing, training or exercising their pets. Walk around them, in role as Rani, asking and learning about caring for different pets. At each place, Rani sneezes once or twice and rubs her eyes.

Finally, bring everyone together to tell them what you, in role as Rani, have decided:

● *I have discovered that I must be allergic to many animals.*

● *I have sneezed while looking at them all.*

● *I would have loved a cuddly guinea-pig, but I just can't have one. It would make me sneeze more and may give me problems breathing.*

● *I must have a pet without fur.*

● *I would love to buy a . . . tank of fish!*

Activity 4   Creating a fish tank

Teacher's intentions

- To provide information about fish aquariums.
- To bring the class together into a shared dramatic representation.

Dramatic construction: creating a fish tank

Explain to the children that together they will create a fish tank with their own bodies. Each part of the fish tank is created in turn. While each part is being planned the others can relax their arms, but remain in the positions as the aspects of the tank.

Teacher, speaking in role as Rani, explains:

You have taught me that I could have sea water fish kept in salt-water, but I would like freshwater tropical fish. I need a tank with glass on four sides.

Organise the children to stand forming the four sides of the rectangular tank with their arms outstretched to make it quite big (perhaps six children on two sides, and two to three children on the other two sides).

I have been told it is very important to have a water filter in the water to keep it clean. Water goes through the filter and comes out cleaner.

Two or three children can stand in the corner making washing actions with their hands to represent the filter.

You have taught me that fish need oxygen in the water so they can breathe. The tank needs oxygenation that sends bubbles of oxygen into the water.

Two children wave and flick their hands as though they are creating bubbles. They can make the sound of bubbles too.

In another corner of the tank we need a heater. The fish I want are tropical fish which need constantly to be in warm water.

A child is positioned to represent the heater, usually a long, thin tube which covers a large expanse of water.

The heater has a thermometer attached to it so that when the water is hot it switches the heater off, and when the water is getting cool it turns the heater on.

A child 'connects' to the heater and creates a signal for when it should turn on and off. It may be open hands or a click sound, or both.

Finally, I can select my fish. I have learned today that some fish like to swim in shoals with the same type of fish. Neon tetras are pretty little fish with two horizontal stripes of colour, such as red and green. They move in groups and keep very close together.

Some of the children move around in the tank in a close-knit group as neon tetras.

List
What do pet owners need to remember to do to look after their pets properly? Make a list.

Websites
Send pet e-cards at http://www.123greetings.com/pets/.
Look up pet care information at http://www.petsathome.com/.

Survey of children's pets
Create a large diagram to match children with their pets. How many are there of each pet?

Growing

Plant hamster food in pots to see what grows. What sorts of seeds do you think they were?

Angel fish are more sedate. They hover, gently propelling themselves with their long, elegant fins. They have black vertical stripes.

Children move differently to be angel fish.

Other fish may be added, such as sucking loach that help keep the tank clean because they eat the green algae that grows on the sides of the tank. They have sucker-like mouths which attach themselves to the glass.

Once the tank has been created you can mime dropping pinches of food flakes on to the water. The children can swap roles so that they learn about the different parts of the tank and the different fish. Finally, Rani thanks the children for their help and advice, and assures them that she will clean the tank regularly and feed the fish daily.

You may like to tell a story about the fish in the tank for the children to act out.

Plenary discussion

Discussion: what we know about . . .

In groups or as a class, list what anyone will need to know if they are thinking of buying a rabbit, a dog, a horse, a fish tank. Include the pets that the children chose in Activity 3.

Matching: which pets need what?

Children make suggestions about a suitable pet for you:

- *I am an old man who can't walk very far. I want some company in my house.*
- *I am a 6-year-old who lives in a flat.*
- *I am a 13-year-old outdoor type who has asthma.*
- *We are a family of five with three children between the ages of 10 and 17.*

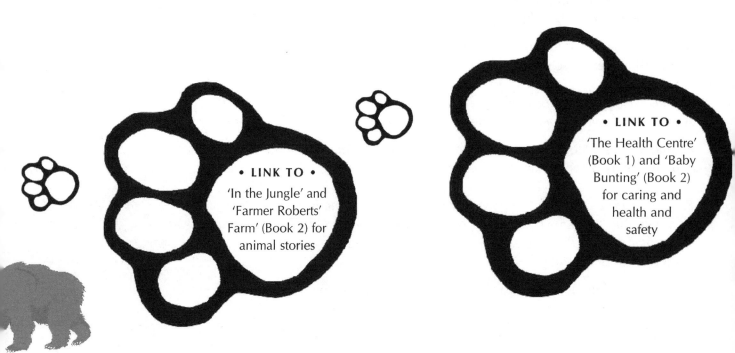

• LINK TO •
'In the Jungle' and 'Farmer Roberts' Farm' (Book 2) for animal stories

• LINK TO •
'The Health Centre' (Book 1) and 'Baby Bunting' (Book 2) for caring and health and safety

All for One and One for All

Yolande and Frank are best friends. Although everyone loves them, they often get up to mischief. They can't help showing off. Frank has a great voice and loves demonstrating his singing, and Yolande can do the most amazing wheelies and spin tricks in her wheelchair. When their class is invited to take part in a huge gym display, their dream is winning the trophy. They shout a slogan for themselves about their shared commitment, 'All for one and one for all'. However, they find that the displays are in an upstairs room with no access for wheelchair users.

Aims

- To invite a consideration of equal opportunities issues.
- To develop a sense of social responsibility.
- To provide the opportunity to practise formal persuasive talk.
- To do exercises in a fictional context.

Themes

- Inclusion.
- Physical activity.
- Community spirit.
- Competition.

Resources

None are necessary, although you may decide to use PE equipment and make the competition entry as realistic as possible.

The imaginative play area can be designed as a gymnasium. This could be an outdoor play area and use outdoor equipment.

Notes

This drama is about children preparing a gym display and about the lack of consideration often given to those with physical disability in terms of access. It also challenges notions of what a child who has a physical disability is expected to do. This girl loves gymnastics. Children get involved with the story of the drama which draws them into considering Yolande's right to equal access at the level of the story which is appropriate for the early years. It is not necessary to bring in broader considerations for those with disabilities, but the drama may be useful to support such areas in personal, social and health education (PSHE).

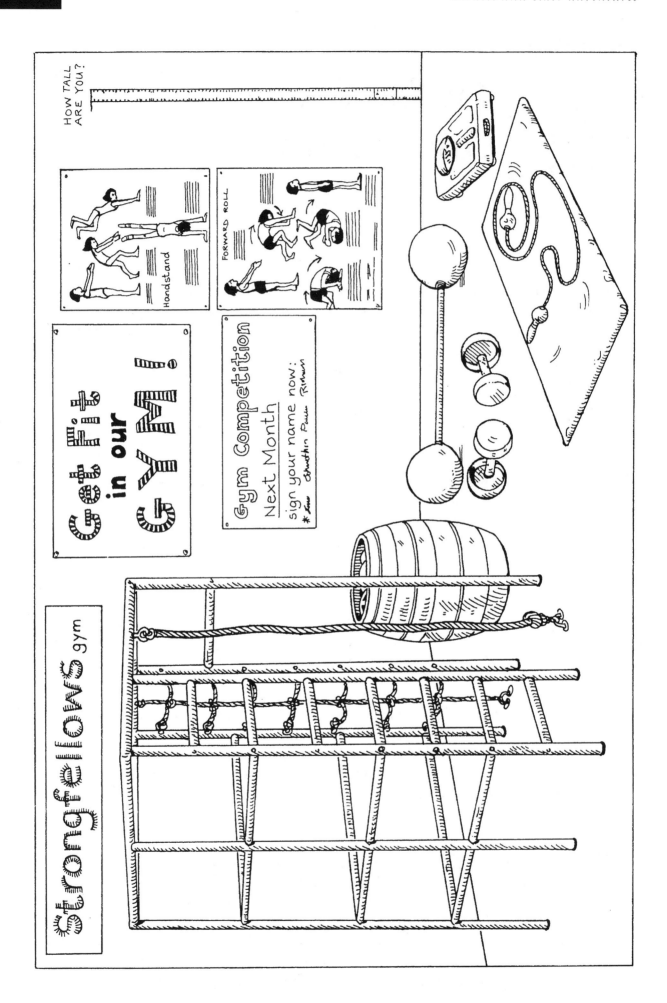

Activity 1 Who are Yolande and Frank?

Teacher's intentions

- To introduce the characters of the drama.
- To develop listening skills.
- To enable each child to make up a statement about imaginary characters.
- To develop affection for the central characters.

Narration: introducing Yolande and Frank

Frank and Yolande are the best of friends. They do everything together. Both children love nothing more than showing off! [Said with a smile!] Frank loves to show off his singing. He has a great voice and is always singing – especially when there's an audience! Yolande uses a wheelchair and adores showing off her wheelie and spinning tricks. She can spin the chair very fast and make it rear up like a horse! It worries her friends sometimes when she rears up too high. But they all know how good she is and they know she shows off to strangers, too!

Yolande and Frank sometimes get into trouble for singing and spinning in the wrong places. Their friends enjoy telling stories of them showing off where they should be still and quiet.

Storytelling: what the two get up to

Where might Yolande and Frank be showing off when they should be quiet? What happened?

Examples include in assembly, in the library, in the supermarket.

Ask the children to imagine they are school friends of Yolande and Frank. They all have some funny stories to tell about them. Like the time when . . . .

The children tell about how the headteacher went pink with anger when Yolande and Frank sang and spun in assembly, or when they drove the wheelchair into a large display in the supermarket.

Gymnastic terms

Demonstrate or show pictures of different gymnastic actions, such as the somersault, cartwheel or handstand; and of equipment, such as a box, horse, trampet, springboard or equipment appropriate to the age of the children.

Character studies

Invite the children to suggest single words to describe the characters of Frank and Yolande (e.g. naughty, fun, lively). Then ask for phrases (e.g. kids who like to have a laugh, risk takers, friends with everyone).

Gymnastics

Plan and prepare a short gym display.

Poster designs

Design posters to advertise a gym display – perhaps their own.

Activity 2   Preparing for a gym display

Teacher's intentions

- To move the drama on.
- To practise physical exercise.

Whole group discussion in role: planning the gym display

Explain to the class that they will pretend to be the children in Frank and Yolande's class. You will be in role as their teacher.

I have some very exciting news for you all. This morning Frank and Yolande are not here because they are receiving prizes for their gym display. You know they had entered the town's competition for pair work. We are keen to build on their success and to enter the big class gym display. This means that all of you will have to think up some ideas and to practise. Yolande and Frank will be so pleased if you all train for the display.

Have you any ideas about what we could do in the display?

Head-over-heels, cartwheels, jumping and skipping, work with hoops.

Exercising: getting fit

A range of exercises may be carried out.

Stretches: reaching up high; reaching out in front; reaching towards your toes.

Arms circles: windmill arms one at a time and then both together. Try them moving in opposite directions.

Jogging on the spot; moving around the space without touching each other.

Remember to mention Frank and Yolande now and again to keep the children in the imagined context:

- *I saw Frank doing this exercise when they were training for their gym display.*
- *Yolande can circle her arms in different directions and then change the direction a few times.*
- *What else have you seen them do?*
- *We must get fit so we don't let them down.*

Still images: practising gymnastics

Ask the children to make still images of things they could do in the gym display. (Still images are safer than performing the gym moves, especially if you are not working with mats). They may wish to work with others or on their own. They will try out different ideas. It doesn't matter if they wouldn't really be able to do them. Once they are all holding their positions, move around them as you narrate:

The children learned that they had to trust each other and that they had to work as one. If one person was not in the right position, it could spoil the next person's move, which would upset the overall effect. They also learned to rely on each other to be where they were needed at the right moment. They used the phrase, 'All for one and one for all' to represent the closeness of the gym team they became over weeks of practising. There were never any absentees from rehearsals because everyone knew that they were all important to the team and for their display.

Activity 3   The big day arrives

Teacher's intentions

- To develop imagination.
- To stimulate empathetic responses.
- To sing in a fictional context.

Narration and making statements: the coach journey

Explain that all the children have to board a coach that will take them to the town where the gym competition is being held. Organise chairs in rows like a coach or agree the space that will represent the coach. Indicate where the step up to the door is.

They were all excited. Some felt they should have practised certain things more, others were excited that their families would be seeing their work, and others still imagined holding the trophy! As they boarded the coach they were silent, thinking of their hopes and fears. Yolande got into the coach first on a special rising platform. She hated the fact that she always had to be in the front near the teachers. Frank usually stayed by her, but she knew that, like her, he would have loved to be on the back seat with other friends.

In role as teacher, tell the children that we will hear what each child was thinking as they got into the coach. Stand by the door to the coach and explain that each person will walk past you, saying out loud what they are thinking, and then climb into the coach and sit down.

Examples might include:

- *I hope I don't fall when I'm upside down.*
- *We will win!*
- *I am excited.*

Singing: in-coach entertainment

Invite a good singer to pretend to be Frank and start the singing. The children can choose the song. 'The Wheels on the Bus Go Round and Round', perhaps. They end each song with a shout: 'All for one and one for all!' This expresses their sense of unity as a gym team which needs to rely on and trust each other.

Singing
Write a short rap telling the story of Frank and Yolande. Sing travelling songs appropriate for the coach journey.

Outfit design
Design a new sports shirt and trainers.

List
Make a list of objects in the school with wheels.

Activity 4   Things go wrong

Teacher's intentions

- To develop responsibility for others.
- To practise formal persuasive language.

Whole group improvisation: organiser's greeting

Explain that you will now enter the coach as the gymnastics display organiser to welcome them all. The children remain sitting as though they are in the coach.

Leave the space and then approach in role. Enter where the door was imagined to be and address the children:

Welcome! I am very pleased to greet you on behalf of all of us involved with the National Gym Competition. Have you had a good journey?

I expect you are all nervous. Here we do have the best gym teams from the schools across the country. But I must not delay you. We don't have a lot of time.

Please leave the coach as quickly as possible. Run over this grassy bank to that spiral staircase at the edge of the building. If you go up three flights and enter through a yellow door, you will find your changing rooms on the left. If you change into your kit in there and then go up to the fourth floor you will find our huge, beautiful gymnasium. You will be shown where to sit.

Could you hurry along now since we have a lot of children to organise? Good luck and enjoy the day.

The children may not need any help to realise that there is a problem for Yolande to get over a grassy bank and up the stairs, but, if they do need help, you might ask who are their trophy winners in the other gym competitions. Or try the prompt: *How long will it take you to get up there and get ready? Are you all fast runners?*

When the children point out that Yolande can't get up a spiral staircase and ask for a lift, the organiser is not very helpful. She tries to avoid the issue:

- *I don't think there's time for any changes.*
- *There isn't a lift in this building.*
- *I'm sorry, but we didn't think about it – now can we go?*

The children argue the case and ask what can be done. The organiser has no idea and suggests that they do their best without Yolande who can stay downstairs! The children may decide that they won't do their gym at all, or that they will do it in a different space on the ground floor and the judges will have to come downstairs to see them.

Storytelling: ending the story

You can discuss with the children how they want the story to end. They usually want the children to win the competition, of course. They may also want a new gymnasium that wheelchair users can comfortably use, or to demand that a lift be fitted.

The children can choose to tell the ending together contributing a sentence in turn, or it can be told by the teacher.

Discussion

About wheelchairs and other aids used by people (e.g. hearing aids, spectacles, walking sticks). If possible, close observation of a wheelchair may help to remove its distance from the experience of many of the children.

Activity 5   Plenary

Teacher's intentions

- To discuss the issues raised in the drama.
- To consider Yolande's feelings.

A discussion should enable the children to reflect on the story and consider the implications of organisations not planning and preparing for everyone, considering only those without disability.

How was Yolande feeling when this conversation went on between the organiser and the children (e.g. *She didn't matter; She was spoiling the team's chances; She won't try gym competitions again; She is very angry...*).

Are there other places you know of that Yolande might have difficulty getting into? In this school? In this town?

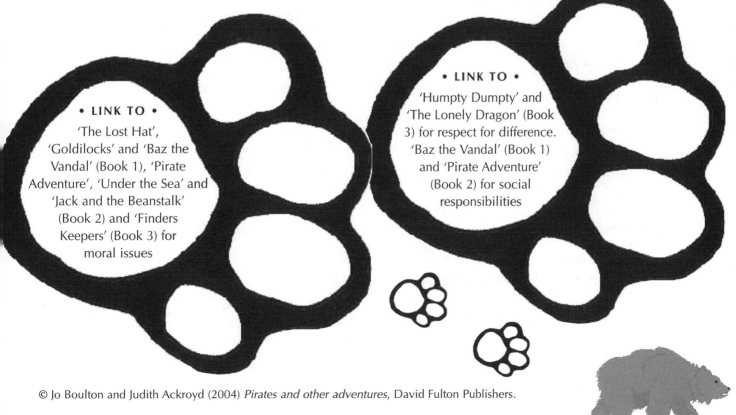

• **LINK TO** •
'The Lost Hat', 'Goldilocks' and 'Baz the Vandal' (Book 1), 'Pirate Adventure', 'Under the Sea' and 'Jack and the Beanstalk' (Book 2) and 'Finders Keepers' (Book 3) for moral issues

• **LINK TO** •
'Humpty Dumpty' and 'The Lonely Dragon' (Book 3) for respect for difference. 'Baz the Vandal' (Book 1) and 'Pirate Adventure' (Book 2) for social responsibilities

7 Farmer Roberts' Farm

Farmer Bob lives alone at Home Farm, which he rents from the local landowner Mrs Billing. He has lived and worked there all his life and loves the animals and the outdoor life. He employs workers to help him at different times of the year such as harvest and haymaking. He is, however, becoming a little forgetful, and needs increasing amounts of help and advice from his employees. Once he forgot to shut a gate and the cows got out on to the road. One of the fences is so rotten that the chickens escape. One day, Farmer Bob receives a letter from Mrs Billing saying she is coming to inspect the farm. She has heard that things are not going well at Home Farm, and Farmer Bob is in danger of losing his home and his livelihood if the inspection goes badly.

On another occasion Farmer Bob asks for the workers' help to build a new shed for his pigs. There are complaints from local people who say there is a terrible smell. The local planning office insists that something is done. Can the workers help Farmer Bob out of trouble again?

Aims

- To find out about the job of a farmer.
- To explore the feelings of someone who is growing old and forgetful.
- To work together to solve the problems.

Themes

- Ageing.
- Helping others.
- Taking care of animals.

Resources

Optional: Hat or coat for Farmer Bob.
Letter from Mrs Billing (see page 60).

The imaginative play area can be designed as a farmyard.

The Manor House

Green Lane

Billing Village

Dear Farmer Roberts,

It has been brought to my attention that things are not as they should be at Home Farm. I have been told that the place is in a terrible mess because you don't keep it clean and tidy enough. I have also been told that you are becoming very forgetful and have left the gate open and forget to shut the barn door. Animals have been escaping on to the road and causing a danger to the traffic. I am very alarmed about this. I will be making an inspection of Home Farm on Friday next week. I will expect to see everything in good order. Otherwise, I will have to consider carefully whether you are a fit person to be the manager at Home Farm. You may have to leave and find somewhere else to live for your retirement. I have the addresses of some retirement homes if you are interested.

Yours sincerely,

Anne Billing

Anne Billing (Mrs)

Activity 1   What do we know about farms and farming?

Teacher's intentions

- To build belief in Home Farm.
- To practise mime.

Discussion: what happens on the farm?

Tell the children that you are going to narrate a story about a farm. Briefly share ideas about farms and what happens on them. Tell them that the farm in the story is called Home Farm. Ask the children to describe the farm. (Use the collective map – see circle activity – as a visual stimulus for this discussion if this has been made previously.)

What kinds of jobs will need to be done at Home Farm? (e.g. feed the chickens, milk the cows, dig the potatoes, sow the grain, harvest the wheat, drive the tractor, muck out the pigs). What do we need to do to keep the animals safe and healthy?

Ask the children to say which are the nice jobs and which are not so pleasant!

Mime: practising jobs on the farm

Stand up in the space. Take a few of the children's suggestions about farm jobs. Ask the children how they would be able to show the job they were doing without talking (e.g. through mime). Ask individual children to show the rest how to mime certain jobs and then encourage everyone to join in. Encourage thoughtful, focused 'realistic' mimes rather than mimes which are rushed and noisy. Ask questions to focus their attention.

What would you be holding in your hands if you were feeding the chickens? Everyone pick up your bag or bucket of feed. Lovely! Show me how heavy it is by the expression on your face. Now take out a handful of feed and throw it gently to the chickens. That's great.

If we are going to milk the cows, what will we do first? Wash our hands? Are we going to do it by hand or will we use a machine?

Discussion

What do farmers do? Have any of the children ever visited a farm? What kind of animals would you expect to find on a farm?

Collective map of the farm

Draw a map of the farm on large sheets of paper. Ask the children to draw the farmhouse, the barn, the henhouse and whatever else they suggest on the map. They can also add land features such as a stream, a duck pond and trees.

Singing game

'The Farmer's in his Den'
Play the original game or use different words as in this version.
1 The Farmer's in his den.
The Farmer's in his den E I E I
The Farmer's in his den.
2 The farmer wants a sheep
3 The farmer wants a horse
4 The farmer wants some hens
5 The farmer wants a dog
6 We all pat the dog

Activity 2   Farmer Bob welcomes his new workers

Teacher's intentions

- To introduce the teacher role of Farmer Bob.
- To develop the children's roles.
- To provide opportunities for the children to ask and answer questions.

Meeting: welcome to Home Farm

Children sit in a circle. Tell the children that you are going to be in role as Farmer Bob in the drama. You may choose to wear a battered old hat or coat to show when you are in role.

Thank you all for coming to work here at Home Farm this summer. Summer is always a busy time for me and I need all the help I can get. I'm not as young and strong as I was and I'm getting a little forgetful. I haven't met all of you so before we get down to work I would like you to introduce yourselves.

Go around the circle and ask all of the workers to introduce themselves. Ask which jobs they would like to do. Comment about how useful they are all going to be as there is so much to do.

Ask them if they have any questions either about him or the farm. Ask a few children to suggest possible questions (e.g. How long has he lived there? How old is he? What animals does he have? What kind of work does he have in mind for them?). Children can work in pairs to think of a few questions. The workers talk to Farmer Bob and ask any questions they may have.

Bob tries to impart as much information as possible when asked the questions:

- *I have lived at Home Farm all my life although I don't own it.*
- *The farm belongs to Mrs Billing who owns a lot of the land around here.*
- *I am getting near to retirement but love the job and my home, and can't bear the thought that one day I will have to leave.*

Still image and speaking in role: jobs on the farm

Teacher asks the children to find a space in the room and to do the mime that goes with their chosen job. Tell them that you will watch them doing their mimes and then shout '*Freeze!*' and clap your hands. This will be their signal to make a frozen picture of the farm and of all of the workers doing their jobs. You will walk around in role as Farmer Bob, chatting to them. Encourage miming to take place for a few minutes before shouting '*Freeze!*'

Farmer Bob goes around speaking to the workers.

- *How are you getting on?*
- *This looks like hard work!*
- *What are you carrying?*
- *Have you seen my sheepdog Johan anywhere?*
- *Do you know what food to give to the pigs?*
- *Have you ever milked a cow before?*
- *Do you know which creature on the farm lays eggs?*

Activity 3   Working on the farm

Teacher's intentions

- To continue to build investment in the farm.
- To introduce the main problem.
- To work in role.

Whole group improvisation: one sunny day at Home Farm

Tell the children that you are going to be in role as Farmer Bob again. Ask the children to make the still picture of the farm (see Activity 2) and say that this time when you clap your hands they will come to life, and they will see what is going on today on the farm. They can talk to each other and interact. Farmer Bob will come and talk to them. Bring the farm to life. Farmer Bob can give advice, offer suggestions and respond to the workers' questions. Follow any of the children's 'stories'. If someone suggests that the chickens have escaped, help them to solve the problem! Allow the improvisation to continue for about five minutes or more, depending on the engagement of the children. Gather them all together for 'lunch' in the barn. Have a chat about what has been happening. Ask workers to share their stories of the morning's events.

Meeting: a letter arrives from Mrs Billing

Farmer Bob produces a letter from his pocket and looks at it rather nervously.

I've just received this letter. I know who it's from. It's Mrs Billing, the lady who owns this farm and all the land. I hardly dare open it. I know she wants to get rid of me.

Farmer Bob can be persuaded to open the letter and read it (see Resource provided).

Farmer Bob has to admit that all of it is true but he does not want to go to a retirement home. What can the children suggest? How can they show Mrs Billing that Home Farm is in a good state of repair?

Write a list of jobs that need to be done, such as mend the fences, paint the barn, clean out the henhouse and so on.

Research

Find out about farm animals. Find out about their needs – food, drink, bedding – and uses (sheep provide wool and meat, cows provide milk, meat and leather).

A story with actions

Tell a story about the farm using as many 'action' and onomatopoeic words as possible so that the children can join in with the actions (e.g. One rainy day (all make raindrops with fingers), Farmer Bob (all bob up and down) was walking slowly (all walk slowly) along the crunchy gravel path (all say crunch, crunch, crunch).

Visit
Visit a farm.

Activity 4   Getting ready for the inspection

Teacher's intentions

- To introduce a new role which will oppose the group.
- To develop persuasive talk.
- To encourage working together to solve the problem.

Dramatic play: preparing

The workers do all the jobs on the list in preparation for the inspection. This will involve imagining carrying wood for the new fences, hammering, sawing and so on. Farmer Bob helps.

Gathering them all together, Farmer Bob thanks his friends for their help and tells them that he has a hospital appointment on Friday when Mrs Billing is coming. He asks them if they will meet her and show her around.

Rhymes and poems

Farm animal rhymes (e.g. 'Old MacDonald Had a Farm', 'Little Bo Peep'.
This Little Puffin by Elizabeth Matterson has a good selection of farm rhymes.

Whole group improvisation: meeting Mrs Billing

Tell the children that in this part of the story you will be in role as Mrs Billing. Check that they understand what they have to do to help Farmer Bob. You could wear a different hat or carry a prop to indicate the change of role. Mrs Billing is not a very kind person and will take a lot of persuasion.

She responds to what the children say along the lines of:

- *Good morning. My name is Mrs Billing. I have come to meet Farmer Bob. Is he here?*
- *Who are all of you?*
- *Oh he's gone to hospital has he? I knew he wasn't well. He'll have to give up the farm.*
- *It's no good. I hear this place is a disgrace. Really filthy and smelly.*
- *You've been helping to tidy it up? Well, you'd better show me around.*

The children show Mrs Billing around the farm and describe what has been done to improve things.

- *Not bad. The fences have been mended very well. I'm sure the animals won't get out now.*
- *This barn certainly looks tidy enough and the farmyard is so clean you could eat your lunch off it!*

Ask the children to sit down and have a chat with you.

I'd like to talk to you about Farmer Bob. I think he should retire. He's too old to look after this farm on his own and you won't be here all the time to help him out. Don't you think he would be better off in a retirement home with other people of his own age?

Farm alphabet
List items that may be found on the farm beginning with the letters of the alphabet. X, Y and Z are difficult!

Encourage the children to discuss Farmer Bob's position. Come to a decision about whether or not Farmer Bob should stay at Home Farm based on their arguments and the quality of their persuasion.

Discussion: plenary

The children can tell Farmer Bob what happened when Mrs Billing visited.

Discuss the two people the children met in the story of Home Farm.

- *Why didn't Farmer Bob want to leave?*
- *What were the good things about Farmer Bob?*
- *What were his worries?*
- *How would you describe Mrs Billing?*
- *What do you think will happen to Farmer Bob in the future?*
- *What will happen at Home Farm?*

Investigate
Investigate breakfast cereals. Prepare a graph to show the children's favourite cereals.

• LINK TO •
'In the Jungle' and 'Helping at the Pet Shop' (Book 2) for animal stories

• LINK TO •
'The Lost Hat', 'Goldilocks' and 'Baz the Vandal' (Book 1) and 'Pirate Adventure', 'Under the Sea' 'Jack and the Beanstalk' and 'All for One and One for All' (Book 2) for stories with moral issues

• LINK TO •
'The Not So Jolly Postman', 'The Park' and 'The Health Centre' (Book 1) for stories about jobs people do

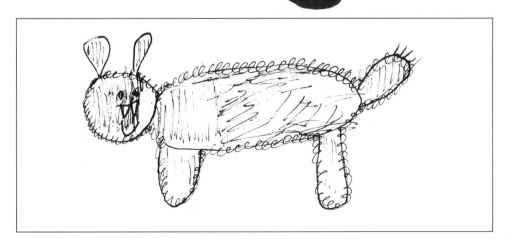

Johan the sheepdog, by Charlie

8 Mary Mary and the Giant

A little girl, Mary, is always called 'Mary Mary' by her family and friends. This is because, like her namesake in the nursery rhyme, she is always contrary. Whatever you say she says the opposite. If you say it is a hot day she'll say it's cold. So when she tells everyone that she is not afraid of the giant who lives on the hill, no one believes her; they think she is just being contrary as usual. One day Mary sets off to visit the giant and takes her friends with her. The children find that he needs help. What is the matter with the giant and can the children help him?

Aims

- To explore the notion that 'appearances can be deceptive'.
- To discuss fears about unknown people and places.

Themes

- Anti-stereotyping.
- Fears.
- Cleanliness.
- Health and safety.
- Trust.

Resources

Optional: Coat or hat for the giant; copy of the book *Mary Mary* by Sarah Hayes.
Copy of the rhyme 'Mary Mary Quite Contrary' (see page 68).

The imaginative play area can be designed as the giant's house, a castle or a garden.

Notes

The stimulus for this drama is a book by Sarah Hayes called *Mary Mary* published by Walker Books. We have taken the basic idea in the book and adapted it. If you are unable to find the book you can still teach the session, since all necessary information for the drama is provided.

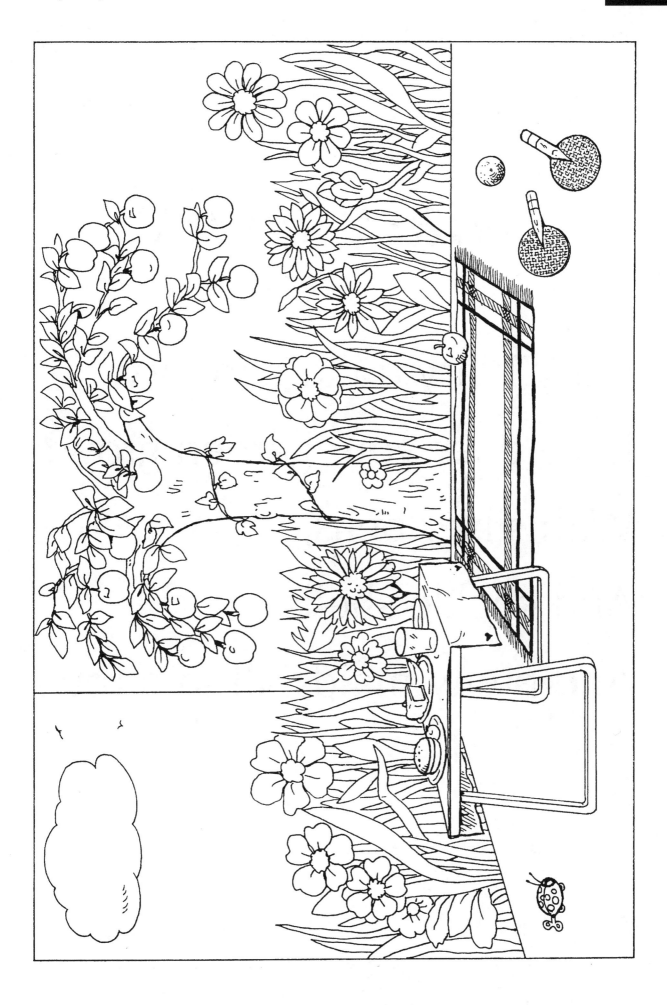

Mary Mary

Mary Mary quite contrary,

How does your garden grow?

With silver bells,

And cockle shells,

And pretty maids all in a row.

Activity 1 Let's tell a story about a giant who lived at the top of a hill

Teacher's intentions

- To set the scene.
- To practise mime.
- To engage in storytelling.

Storytelling or reading: setting the scene

Either read the opening page of the book or tell a version of the opening as follows:

Mary Mary who was, as we know, always contrary and said the opposite of anything you said and did the opposite of anything you did, lived in a town at the bottom of a hill. At the top of the hill was a huge house where a giant lived. The people in the town were terrified of the giant.

Discuss with the children why the people were afraid.

Lead a storytelling session about the town and what the people say about the giant. Be careful to emphasise that these things were said to have happened but no one really knows.

All the people in the village knew there was a giant living in a huge house at the top of the hill. They often saw him . . . and sometimes he was . . . . If the giant ever came down to the village the people . . . because they thought he might . . . . He never managed to speak to anyone because . . .

End with:

But Mary Mary was not afraid of anyone or anything and was certainly not afraid of any old giant. One day she decided to go up to the giant's house and see him. She asked her friends to go with her. They weren't afraid either.

Narration and mimed action: going up the hill to the giant's house

Ask the children to join in with the actions as you narrate the journey up the hill to the giant's house.

So they put on their coats and gloves and scarves and opened the doors to their houses. They walked quickly across the town until they came to the hill. It was quite steep and they began to walk slower and slower. They climbed over rocks and used branches from the trees to help to pull them up the hill. They waded through the long grass and jumped over the stream. They were getting tired now and had a short sit-down on a tree trunk. Eventually they reached the doorstep of the house. It was enormous. How were they going to get up?

Ask for the children's suggestions.

- *That's a good idea. They tried to jump but it was too high.*
- *They tried to climb but they slipped back down.*
- *They found a rock to stand on and finally they heaved themselves on to the step.*
- *There in front of them was the giant's door. It was ENORMOUS! They stepped up and knocked hard three times. After a while they heard the key turn in the lock and the door began to creak open.*

© Jo Boulton and Judith Ackroyd (2004) *Pirates and other adventures*, David Fulton Publishers.

Nursery rhyme
Read and learn the rhyme.
What does 'contrary' mean?
Have you ever been contrary?

Opposites
Practise saying opposites.
Teacher: *When I say huge Mary Mary says . . .*
Children: *Tiny.*
Teacher: *When I say hot Mary Mary says . . .*
Children: *Cold.*

Stories about giants
Make a collection of stories about giants such as:
Jack and the Beanstalk Traditional
The Selfish Giant Oscar Wilde
Jim and the Beanstalk Raymond Briggs
The Teddy Robber Ian Beck

Activity 2   Why is the giant sad?

Teacher's intentions

- To introduce the teacher in role as the giant.
- To talk to the teacher in role as the giant.
- To introduce the problem.

Hot seating: meeting the giant

When the door opened the giant was standing there nervously. He looked very sad and was in a terrible mess. His hair was so long he couldn't see through it, his clothes were dirty and falling to pieces. He spoke in a hoarse voice and his eyes were filled with tears.

Tell the children that you are going to be in role as the giant in the next part of the story. Use an old coat or hat to wear or hold to indicate when you are in role. The children are going to be able to talk to the giant and find out why he is so sad. Ask the children to think of some questions they might ask the giant. His worries gradually emerge:

- *The people are frightened of me when I come to the village, so they won't let me into the shops to buy any cleaning equipment.*
- *My clothes have fallen into rags but even if they would let me into the shop the clothes are too small for me.*
- *I'm a mess and my house and garden are also in a mess.*
- *I am lonely and miserable without friends to talk to.*

The children will offer or the giant asks the children to help him tidy up himself and his house.

Mary Mary, by Charlie

Activity 3   Managing the giant

Teacher's intentions

- To give children responsibility for suggesting what should be done.
- To involve the children in still image work and dramatic play.
- To solve the problem.

Meeting: deciding what needs to be done

The teacher leads a discussion about what jobs will need to be done. Make a list of jobs that need doing. Ask individual children what they would like to do to help the giant. What equipment will need to be used? Make a list of the items that need to be bought in the village. Encourage the use of verbs – sweeping, polishing, vacuuming, cleaning. Make a list of things that the giant needs to do for himself (e.g. wash his face, brush his hair, clean his teeth, put on clean clothes).

The children could enact going to the village shop and buying household equipment for the giant. Alternatively, older children could work in groups of three. One is the shopkeeper, one is the giant and one is the giant's friend. The giant's friend must persuade the shopkeeper to let the giant in to buy equipment.

Write a list
List verbs to record what was done to help the giant to manage himself (e.g. clean, polish, sweep, wash).

Still image: cleaning the giant's house

Ask the children to choose a job they would like to do in the giant's house. Ask them to stand in a space and practise doing their job. When you clap your hands they can freeze, and in role as the giant you can go round and talk to them about what they have been doing and what they think of the mess you are in.

- *What have you been doing to help me?*
- *You're so kind.*
- *What do you think I can do about my hair? It's such a mess.*
- *Do you really think I need a bath?*
- *Mary Mary says I'm smelly, but it doesn't matter, does it?*

Word storm...
Words to describe giants.

Dramatic play: this is hard work!

Children can set to work to clean up the house and garden if suggested. Teacher in role as the giant goes around to talk and ask questions about what they are doing, helping where necessary.

Narration: a surprise invitation

The giant was so pleased with the help that the children had given him that he planned a surprise for them. He sent them all home with a letter inviting them to the opening of a new children's playground in his garden. The Grand Opening would take place the following week and everyone from the town was invited.

Discuss how the children would be feeling about this.

© Jo Boulton and Judith Ackroyd (2004) *Pirates and other adventures*, David Fulton Publishers.

Design a playground

What things would there be in your ideal playground? Discuss and draw.

Activity 4   The Mayor presents a challenge

Teacher's intentions

- To introduce a challenging role.
- To encourage children to use persuasive language.
- To discuss fear of the unknown.

Meeting and discussion in role: the Mayor is not amused

Tell the children that the children in the town have been asked to talk to the Mayor about what happened at the giant's house.

Teacher in role as Mayor welcomes the children and questions them about what happened. She is clearly angry that the children have been to visit the giant and tells them that they are not to go again. At first, she will not listen to their arguments and will not give permission for them to attend the opening of the playground. The children have to use all of their powers of persuasion to change her mind. They are eventually successful and she says they can go so long as she can go too to make sure all is well.

Discussion: what will the playground be like?

Ask the children to describe the best pieces of equipment in children's playgrounds and how they are used.

Activity 5   At the giant's playground

Teacher's intentions

- To bring the playground to life.
- To enable a satisfactory ending to the story.
- To use descriptive language.

Story map
Record the order of events in the story on a timeline or story map.

Narration and mime: the Grand Opening of the playground

Children mime the events as they are described.

The day of the Grand Opening arrived. The children woke up early and stretched. They all felt very excited and had a funny feeling in their tummies like butterflies fluttering around. They got dressed in their play clothes and put on their trainers. They opened their doors and began to walk up the hill towards the giant's house. When they arrived, they saw that the side gate was open and they walked through into the giant's garden. It was amazing! A big sign said 'Welcome to your playground. Thank you for your help!' The children stood very still and looked around. They couldn't see the giant but they could see the best playground for children that had ever been made.

Still image and dramatic play: playing in the playground

Ask individual children to go and stand near something in the playground they want to play on. Tap each on the shoulder and ask questions:

- *What are you going to play on? What colour is it? How high is the slide?*
- *How do you feel about this playground?*

Discussion
Discuss childhood fears. The people in the town were afraid of the giant. What scares you?

Children play in the playground and teacher in role as Mayor goes around chatting to them.

Discussion: plenary

- How had the giant got himself into such a terrible state?
- Was it his fault?
- What did they do to help him?
- Why was the Mayor so angry with the children?
- How did the children persuade him?
- Why wasn't the giant there at the opening of the playground?
- What happened next in the story?

• LINK TO •
'Jack and the Beanstalk' (Book 2) for giant stories

• LINK TO •
'Pirate Adventures' (Book 2) and 'The Lonely Dragon' (Book 3) for stories about confronting fears and anti-stereotyping

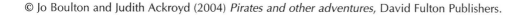

© Jo Boulton and Judith Ackroyd (2004) *Pirates and other adventures*, David Fulton Publishers.

CHAPTER 9 Cinderella

Ella, or Cinderella as her two nasty sisters call her, is a rather sad and weak girl. The children meet her, and are able to give her advice about dealing with and standing up to her bullying sisters. When an invitation arrives inviting all the girls to the Prince's birthday party at the palace, her two sisters tell Ella that she can't go as there is too much work to do at home. Ella does go to the party but in this version of the story it is not because of a fairy godmother. Ella's friends help to give her confidence and show her useful strategies for increasing her self-esteem. She manages to persuade her sisters to allow her to go to the party where she decides whether or not to marry the Prince.

Aims

- To use a traditional tale as a starting point.
- To explore bullying.
- To practise assertive and persuasive language.

Themes

- Fairytales.
- Bullying.
- Sibling rivalry.

Resources

Optional: Large sheet of paper and felt-tip pens; apron for Cinderella; hat or shawl for sisters.

The imaginative play area can be designed as a kitchen, a palace ballroom or a castle.

Notes

This drama takes a twist on the traditional Cinderella story. It is useful but not essential that the children have heard the traditional version before doing the drama, but not immediately before the lesson. The traditional story introduces Cinderella's sisters as stepsisters and the mother is a stepmother. You might prefer to leave this out. The drama will explore the issue of sibling rivalry, but does not set out to deal with issues of reconstituted families unless this comes directly from the children.

Word shower
Happy and sad words.

Activity 1   What is the matter with the girl?

Teacher's intentions

- To use mime as an introduction.
- To introduce the teacher in role as Cinderella.
- To focus on body language and facial expression.

Mime: what can we tell about this person by watching a mime?

Tell the children that they are going to watch you doing a mime. You are Cinderella but don't tell the children! Include some of the following:

Pick up a broom and begin to sweep the floor. Polish, dust clean. Carry a heavy bucket of coal. Wipe your forehead. Sigh. Look downcast and unhappy. Rub your hands near the fire to warm them. Sit down close to the fire and go to sleep.

Talk to the children about who you were and what you were doing.

- *What did they see?*
- *What was the person doing?*
- *Who was the person in the mime?*
- *How was the person feeling?*
- *How do we know?*

The children may instantly recognise who it is but try to draw out how we know she is feeling sad. Focus on the body language and facial expressions.

Art
Draw pictures of a happy Cinderella and a sad Cinderella. Discuss what makes her happy and sad.

Hot seating: what can we find out by talking to her?

Tell the children that they will be able to talk to Ella. How will they approach a sad girl? What do they want to find out? Frame some questions together. Information is be given by the teacher in role:

- *My name is Ella but everyone calls me Cinderella because I usually fall asleep in the hearth by the fire, in among the cinders. That's why my sisters call me Cinderella.*
- *I don't mind because it's lovely and warm there.*
- *I'm so tired because I do all the work in the house.*
- *My mother and sisters are rather lazy but I don't mind doing the work. It's fun.*

Recap on what has been learned about Cinderella. The information is jotted down on paper as a reminder.

Activity 2   The story begins

Teacher's intentions

- To retell part of the story of Cinderella.
- To focus on the characters of the sisters.
- To use thought tapping.

Storytelling, mime and thought tapping: will you help me to tell the story?

Discuss the different characters of Cinderella and her sisters. Use adjectives to describe them. Ask the children to mime the story of Cinderella as you tell it. They will do this individually so will be in role as all the different characters. Your story should be descriptive enough to enable them to portray easily the differences in the characters and should use some of the children's words.

Once there was a girl called Cinderella. She worked very hard all day long in the kitchen, sweeping the floor, washing the dishes, polishing the ornaments, putting coal on the fire... (use ideas from the hot seating section in Activity 1).

Ask the children to freeze and then thought tap them.

- *How do you feel about doing all the work in the house?*
- *Don't you think your sisters should do more to help?*
- *Why do they make you do everything?*

Then continue with the story:

Cinderella's sisters were older than her and not very nice. One was tall and looked angry all the time. She stamped around the house shaking her fist at Cinderella. The other was short with rounded shoulders. She always frowned and never smiled. She always shook her head at Cinderella and wagged her finger at her to make her work harder.

Ask the children to freeze, and again, thought tap them this time as the sisters.

- Why don't you ever help Cinderella to do the work?
- Why are you so unkind to her?

Continue with the story until:

One day an invitation arrived from the palace. The Prince was having a party to celebrate his birthday and was inviting all the girls in the land. You see, he wanted to find a girl to marry! Cinderella and her sisters looked at the invitation excitedly. But then the sisters said to Cinderella, 'Well, don't get so excited, Cinderella. You are not going. The Prince would not want a dirty girl like you there. He wants to marry beautiful girls like us.'

Storytelling
Tell or read the story of Cinderella. Tell the story from the viewpoint of one of the characters.

Collection...
Of different versions of the story. There are many websites offering different versions of the story.

Role on the wall

Draw an outline of one of the three characters. Collect words to describe the characters of either Cinderella or her sisters or all of them.

Activity 3   What can Cinderella do?

Teacher's intentions

● To encourage the children to offer ways for Cinderella to stand up to her sisters.

● To reflect on people who are bullies and what should be done about them.

● To practise using voice and body language to express a point of view.

Circle of thoughts: how does Cinderella feel?

Ask the children to sit in a circle. Discuss:

● *What does Cinderella want to do?*

● *Why won't her sisters let her go to the party?*

● *Why are they treating her like this?*

You can put a chair in the middle to represent Cinderella or you could sit in the middle in role. Ask the children to imagine what Cinderella is feeling at this point in the story.

Ask them to voice aloud her thoughts around the circle.

● *I feel sad.*

● *I want to go to the party.*

● *They can't stop me.*

● *I think they're mean and horrid.*

Discussion: what can she say to make them change their minds?

Tell the children that in this story there is no fairy godmother to make it all right! If Cinderella wants to go to the party she must think of how to stand up to her sisters and persuade them to let her go. Take their ideas.

Teacher in role: helping Ella to be assertive!

Tell the children that you are going to be in role as Ella and they are going to tell you their ideas about how to persuade the sisters. Be quiet, shy and reluctant to be assertive. Ask the children to show you how to act. Remember that assertive doesn't mean aggressive but it is important to get over your point of view calmly! The focus is on tone, volume, body language and use of persuasive language.

● *I couldn't ask my sisters if I can go. I'm too nervous.*

● *What shall I say?*

● *How should I say it?*

● *Like this?* [Shouting]

● *That's no good, they'll shout back.*

Try to encourage suggestions about what could really be said to bullies to make them stop, e.g. telling someone else about the problem (father/mother/the Prince?). The children prepare the teacher in role to solve her own problem.

So Cinderella took the children's advice and went to speak to her sisters.

Thought bubbles

Add bubbles to the sad and happy pictures of Cinderella. What is she thinking and feeling?

Activity 4   The party

Teacher's intentions

- To give feedback to the children.
- To enable the children to evaluate the effectiveness of their suggestions.

Teacher in role discussion: what happened?

Tell the children that the meeting has taken place and Cinderella is coming to tell the children how it went.

[Excitedly] *Well, you'll never guess! I said exactly what you told me about . . .* [use ideas the children suggested] *and they said I could go. They weren't very happy about it. They took some persuading but they said I was right.*

The only problem is that I have nothing to wear! What should I wear to a party at the palace? A dress? Silver slippers? Oh I could never buy any of those things. I haven't got much money.

Take children's suggestions (e.g. borrow a dress, alter an old one, they may offer to give you one or make one). Ask them to describe how you look in your new dress.

Thought tunnel: on the way to the party

Discuss how Cinderella is feeling now – happy, nervous, excited, and can't wait to get there?

Children stand in two lines facing each other. Teacher in role as Cinderella walks along the path to the party. Children speak her thoughts as she passes them.

- *I'm really scared about meeting the Prince.*
- *I want to dance.*
- *I'm excited.*
- *What will there be to eat?*

Whole group improvisation: at the party

You may decide to allocate specific roles to children for this activity: King, Queen, Prince, sisters, guests. Discuss what would happen at the party (e.g. drinking, chatting, dancing, playing games, eating). Ask the children to set up the party scene. This could be done as a still image which is brought to life. Teacher in role as Cinderella enters the scene and walks around meeting people. This activity can go on for as long as you want depending on the involvement of the children.

Discussion: plenary

How did the party end? The children may choose the traditional ending or suggest an alternative. The children must decide whether or not Ella chooses to marry the Prince. Each child can say *Yes* or *No* and could provide a reason.

Talk about the situation of Cinderella and her sisters. Discuss what to do if someone is mean to you.

© Jo Boulton and Judith Ackroyd (2004) *Pirates and other adventures*, David Fulton Publishers.

Design . . .
A dress for Cinderella to wear to the party.

Plan the party
Discuss how the room would be set out. What food, drink and music would there be?

Video
Watch sections of the Disney cartoon version of Cinderella.

To marry or not to marry?
List what Ella's sisters might want in a husband, and then do the same for Ella.

• LINK TO •

'Goldilocks' (Book 1), 'Jack and the Beanstalk' (Book 2) and 'Billy Goats Gruff' and 'Forest Adventure' (Book 3) for traditional tales

10 Under the Sea

There are all sorts of extraordinary creatures living on the reef under the sea. The plankton is dinner for the small fish and the small fish are dinner for the sharks and whales. Life is about knowing who might be after you, and enjoying the colours, the bubbles, the coral and the space of being under the sea. When visitors come from *above* the sea, they are unknown. Are they to be trusted? Should underwater creatures swim away fast, or could these visitors be bringing something good? A timid mermaid has been spotted by the divers who wish to take her to their world to prove that mermaids exist. Should she go with them or stay in the safety of the reef?

Aims

- To learn about the mermaid as a mythical creature.
- To consider moral implications of extending human knowledge.
- To consider life under the sea.

Themes

- The sea.
- Mythical creatures.
- Trust.
- Friendship.

Resources

Optional: Suitable cloak for the mermaid in sea colours.

The imaginative play area can be designed as an underwater scene.

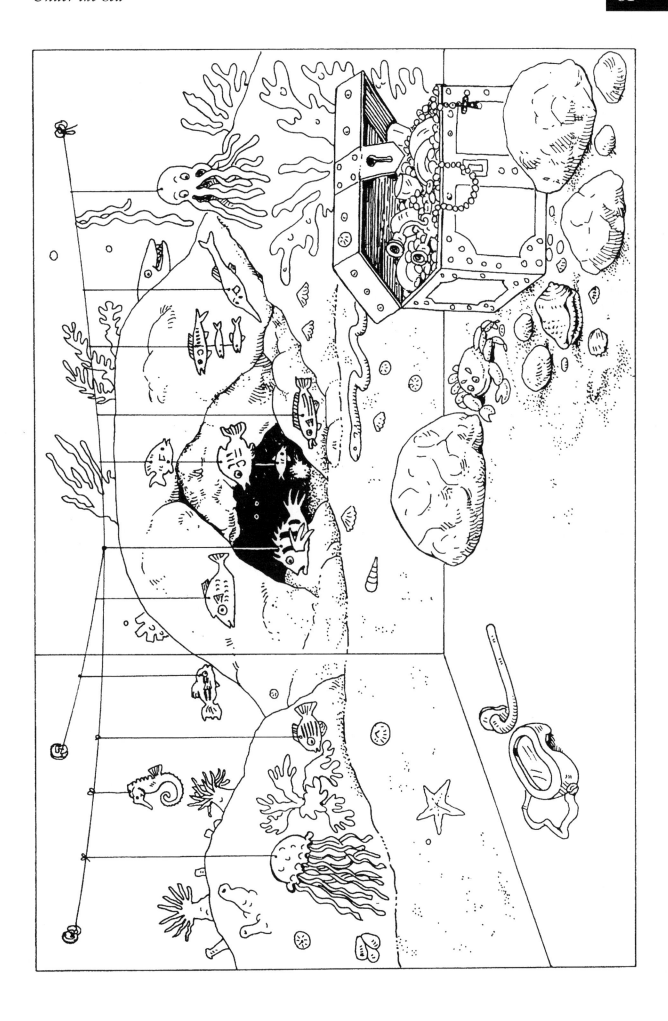

Three-dimensional collage

Children collect artefacts associated with the sea and make large collages by sticking items on to a board, such as shells and sand.

Underwater mobiles

Outlines of fish can be given out to young children to colour. They are then hung up to create a shoal of fish mobile.

Observational drawings

Arrange shells and other sea artefacts or perhaps snorkels and goggles for children to draw.

Activity 1   Introducing what's under the sea

Teacher's intentions

- To introduce the theme.
- To learn the names of some underwater creatures.

Game: The Ocean

This game is played like 'Fruit Bowl' (see 'Games', p. 98), but with sea world names rather than fruit.

The children sit on chairs in a circle. Each is allocated one of three names (e.g. crab, lobster or octopus). A caller in the middle calls out one of the names (e.g. crab), and all the crabs have to leave their seats and find another chair to sit on. The caller's aim is to sit on a chair too. Whoever is left without a chair is the caller in the middle. If 'Ocean' is called, everyone has to leave their chairs and find another one.

Game: Who Eats Who in the Sea

This could be played outside.

Designate the space into four corners or zones and allocate one of the following to each child: killer whales; sharks; flounders; plankton. Explain that killer whales will eat sharks for food, sharks will eat flounders and flounders will eat plankton. The teacher calls out any two names at a time and the groups must leave their corner and move into the corner vacated by the other group. However, if one group eats the other they try to catch them before they enter their new space. Thus, to a call 'killer whales and sharks', the two groups attempt to swap zones, but the killer whales try to catch the sharks. The catching should be done gently! If they are caught, they join the plankton. In the end, most will have become plankton and the children who have managed to stay as sharks or flounders are the winners. Whales will have survived, since no one eats them.

Activity 2   Where the mermaid lives

Teacher's intentions

- To encourage imagination.
- To develop descriptive language.

Shared description: the mermaid's cave

Discuss the children's understanding of mermaids.

Deep down in a warm part of the ocean bed is a beautiful, colourful cave. It is the home of a mermaid. Many sea creatures visit the cave, because they all love to spend time with the mermaid. She is very kind and friendly, and always welcoming. The cave is wonderful. She has collected many objects from the sea bed. Some are useful to her, such as the shells in which she serves her friends juice. Others are purely decorative. The cave has very special colours, too.

- *What colours might be in the mermaid's cave?*
- *What objects has she collected?*
- *What are they used for?*
- *Why is it such a lovely place to be?*

If you have pictures of the sea bed, they will be helpful to stimulate the children's imaginations for this activity.

Invite the children to describe the mermaid's cave as though they are starting a story from a book. They can say a line each after your introductory line: *Deep down in a warm part of the ocean bed is a beautiful, colourful cave. It is the home of a mermaid.*

You may need to provide more narrative for younger children. An example might be:

The walls were covered in shells of all colours. There were . . . ones and . . . ones and some very bright . . . ones. On the floor there were lots of plants. Some looked like stars; others looked like . . . , and others like . . . .

The children will have many imaginative ideas about what the cave is like.

Junk modelling
Create an underwater world with a shipwreck and coral reef.

Knowledge and understanding/ science
Experiment with water and salt. Leave a small metal item, such as a coin, in a jar of water with salt and another without. Observe the difference over time.

Collective drawing
Draw a collective picture of a mermaid or merman.

© Jo Boulton and Judith Ackroyd (2004) *Pirates and other adventures*, David Fulton Publishers.

Activity 3   Why is the mermaid afraid?

Teacher's intentions

- To provide an opportunity to practise questioning skills.
- To introduce the dilemma.
- To encourage children to develop thinking and deductive skills.

Hot seating: the mermaid's problem

The mermaid's friends were surprised that she was not playing with the sea-horses as she usually did early in the mornings. No one had seen her, so they went to her cave. They found her packing a small bag. She invited them all to sit down, and they watched her for a while and then began to ask her what was going on. Why was she packing? Why wasn't she playing out in the bubbles of the blowfish?

The children ask the mermaid questions. Teacher in role as the mermaid (or merman) replies with small pieces of information so that the children have to ask more questions. You need to show that she is worried. Gradually let them know the situation:

- *Some humans from above the water have found me.*
- *They have legs, strange goggles on their faces and large tanks on their backs.*
- *They were amazed to see me because they said that no one living above the water believes that mermaids are real. There they believe they exist only in stories.*
- *They want to take me away with them to show everybody that mermaids are real.*
- *On the one hand, I would love to prove that mermaids are real. On the other hand, I am afraid.*
- *What will happen when I leave the sea water? I have heard that when mermaids go on to land they become human. I think I would like to be human but I'm not sure.*
- *What will they do with me? Will I be put in a tank and never allowed to come home?*

The children may advise the mermaid to stay with them and hide from the divers/humans. They may offer to go with her to protect her. The mermaid indicates that the humans are really not interested in her. They are only interested to show off their discovery.

Activity 4   Plenary

- Have humans brought other objects from the sea? What have you seen? Perhaps there are sea-horses, sea anemones and shells on the nature table.
- Have you seen sea creatures in tanks or large aquariums?
- Do you believe that the mermaid would be brought back to her cave?
- What would you advise the mermaid to do?

Mermaids are not real. There aren't any in the real world, only in books, stories, songs and films. What other creatures are mythical, not in real life? Have you heard of Neptune, the King of the sea? Unicorns? Dragons? Ogres? Giants?

Songs

Listen to songs, such as 'Under the Sea' from Disney's *The Little Mermaid*. Sing sea-shanties.

Music

Create sounds of the sea. This could be through use of the voice only or with percussion instruments. You can conduct the children through from calm to storm and to the stillness after the storm.

Disney film

The Little Mermaid provides wonderful fun scenes of fictional life under the sea. The 'Under the Sea' song brings in lots of different types of sea creatures which are named in the song, such as clams, bass and blowfish. The children can learn to name them as they appear on the screen.

Visits

Visit the seaside or a wet fish shop or fish market.

Knowledge and understanding/ science

Collect items from the seaside and under the sea. Display and label sea-horses, shells, driftwood, seaweed and coral.

Internet research

www.geocities.com/Athens/Atrium/5924/underthesea.htm
This site explores marine biology for elementary classes. It is an attractive, user-friendly site which includes online games and puzzles and lots of information.
www.Germantown.k12.il.us/html/sea.html
Although this site is designed for older children, it provides some beautiful pictures and easily accessible information which will be useful with early years classes.

• LINK TO •
'The Park' and 'Baz the Vandal' (Book 1), 'In the Jungle' (Book 2) and 'The Red Garden' (Book 3) for environmental issues

• LINK TO •
'Pirate Adventure' (Book 2) for sea stories

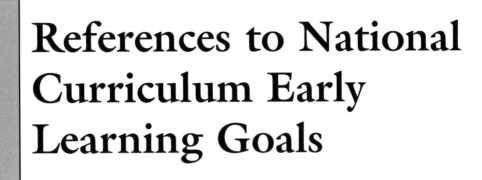

References to National Curriculum Early Learning Goals

EARLY LEARNING GOALS

		CHAPTER									
		1	2	3	4	5	6	7	8	9	10
Personal, social and emotional development											
1	Continue to be interested, excited and motivated to learn.	•	•	•	•	•	•	•	•	•	•
2	Be confident to try new activities, initiate ideas and speak in a familiar group.	•	•	•	•	•	•	•	•	•	•
3	Maintain attention, concentrate, and sit quietly when appropriate.	•	•	•	•	•	•	•	•	•	•
4	Respond to significant experiences, showing a range of feelings when appropriate.	•	•	•	•	•	•	•	•	•	•
5	Have a developing awareness of one's own needs, views and feelings and be sensitive to the needs, views and feelings of others.	•	•	•	•	•	•	•	•	•	•
7	Form good relationships with adults and peers.	•	•	•	•	•	•	•	•	•	•
8	Work as part of a group or class, taking turns and sharing fairly; understand that there need to be agreed values and codes of behaviour for groups of people, including adults and children, to work together harmoniously.	•	•	•	•	•	•	•	•	•	
9	Understand what is right, what is wrong, and why.	•	•	•	•	•	•	•	•	•	•
10	Consider the consequences of one's words and actions for oneself and others.	•	•	•	•	•	•	•	•	•	•
13	Understand that people have different needs, views, cultures and beliefs that need to be treated with respect.	•	•	•	•	•	•	•	•	•	•
14	Understand that one can expect others to treat one's needs, views, cultures and beliefs with respect.	•	•	•	•	•	•	•	•	•	•

EARLY LEARNING GOALS

	CHAPTER									
	1	2	3	4	5	6	7	8	9	10
Communication, language and literacy										
1 Interact with others, negotiating plans and activities and taking turns in conversation.	•	•	•	•	•	•	•	•	•	•
2 Enjoy listening to and using spoken and written language, and readily turn to it in play and learning.	•	•	•	•	•	•	•	•	•	•
3 Sustain attentive listening, responding to what one has heard with relevant comments, questions or actions.	•	•	•	•	•	•	•	•	•	•
4 Listen with enjoyment, and respond to stories, songs and other music, rhymes and poems, and make up one's own stories, songs, rhymes and poems.	•	•	•	•	•	•	•	•	•	•
5 Extend their vocabulary, exploring the meanings and sounds of new words.	•	•	•	•	•	•	•	•	•	•
6 Speak clearly and audibly with confidence and control and show awareness of the listener, for example by their use of conventions such as greetings.	•	•	•	•	•	•	•	•	•	•
7 Use language to imagine and re-create roles and experiences.	•	•	•	•	•	•	•	•	•	•
8 Use talk to organise, sequence and clarify thinking, ideas, feelings and events.	•	•	•	•	•	•	•	•	•	•
13 Retell narratives in the correct sequence, drawing on language patterns of stories.	•	•	•	•	•	•	•	•	•	•
16 Show an understanding of the elements of stories, such as main character, sequence of events…and to answer questions about where, who, why and when.	•	•	•	•	•	•	•	•	•	•
Knowledge and understanding										
4 Ask questions about why things happen and how things work.						•				
9 Observe, find out and identify features in the place where they live and the natural world.	•						•			•
10 Find out about their environment and talk about those features they like and dislike.	•		•				•			

EARLY LEARNING GOALS

	CHAPTER									
	1	2	3	4	5	6	7	8	9	10
Physical development										
1 Move with confidence, imagination and in safety.	•					•				
2 Move with control and coordination.	•					•				
4 Show awareness of space, of themselves and of others.	•					•				
5 Recognise the importance of keeping healthy and those things which contribute to this.	•	•				•		•		
6 Recognise the changes that happen to their bodies when they are active.						•				
Creative development										
2 Recognise and explore how sounds can be changed, sing simple songs from memory…match movements to music.	•	•	•				•	•	•	•
3 Use imagination in art and design, music, dance, imaginative and role play and stories.	•	•	•	•	•		•	•	•	•
5 Express and communicate ideas, thoughts and feelings by using…imaginative and role play…movement.	•	•	•	•	•	•	•	•	•	•

NATIONAL CURRICULUM KEY STAGE 1

	CHAPTER									
	1	2	3	4	5	6	7	8	9	10
En1 Speaking and listening										
1 Speaking										
a speak clear diction and appropriate intonation	•	•	•	•	•	•	•	•	•	•
b choose words with precision	•	•	•	•	•	•	•	•	•	•
c organise what they say	•	•	•	•	•	•	•	•	•	•
d focus on the main points	•	•	•	•	•	•	•	•	•	•
e include relevant detail	•	•	•	•	•	•	•	•	•	•
f take into account the needs of the listener	•	•	•	•	•	•	•	•	•	•
2 Listening										
a sustain concentration	•	•	•	•	•	•	•	•	•	•
b remember specific points that interest them	•	•	•	•	•	•	•	•	•	•
c make relevant comments	•	•	•	•	•	•	•	•	•	•
d listen to others' reactions	•	•	•	•	•	•	•	•	•	•
e ask questions to clarify their understanding	•	•	•	•	•	•	•	•	•	•
3 Group discussion and interaction										
a take turns in speaking	•	•	•	•	•	•	•	•	•	•
b relate their contribution to what has gone before	•	•	•	•	•	•	•	•	•	•
c take different views into account	•	•	•	•	•	•	•	•	•	•
d extend their ideas in the light of discussion	•	•	•	•	•	•	•	•	•	•
e give reasons for opinions and actions	•	•	•	•	•	•	•	•	•	•

NATIONAL CURRICULUM KEY STAGE 1

		CHAPTER									
		1	2	3	4	5	6	7	8	9	10
4	**Drama**										
a	use language and actions to explore and convey situations, characters and emotions	•	•	•	•	•	•	•	•	•	•
b	create and sustain roles individually and when working with others	•	•	•	•	•	•	•	•	•	•
c	comment constructively on drama they have watched or in which they have taken part	•	•	•	•	•	•	•	•	•	•
6	**Language variation**										
a	pupils should be taught how speech varies in different circumstances	•	•	•	•	•	•	•	•	•	•
b	to take account of different listeners	•	•	•	•	•	•	•	•	•	•
	Sc2 Science										
2b	humans and other animals need food and water to stay alive	•	•			•					
e	how to treat animals with care and sensitivity					•		•			
f	that humans and other animals can produce offspring and that these offspring grow into adults		•			•		•			
4a	recognise similarities and differences between ourselves and others, and to treat others with sensitivity		•			•					•
5c	to care for the environment	•						•			•
	Physical education										
8a	perform basic skills in travelling, being still, finding space and using it safely						•				
d	create and perform short, linked sequences that show a clear beginning, middle and end						•				
	Geography										
2e	make maps and plans			•							
3a	identify and describe what places are like	•			•				•		•

NATIONAL CURRICULUM KEY STAGE 1

	CHAPTER									
	1	2	3	4	5	6	7	8	9	10
PSHE and citizenship										
1a to recognise what they like and dislike, what is fair and unfair, and what is right and wrong	•		•	•		•	•	•	•	•
b to share their opinions on things that matter to them and explain their views	•	•	•	•	•	•	•	•	•	•
c to recognise, name and deal with their feelings in a positive way	•	•	•	•		•	•	•	•	•
2a to take part in discussions with one other person and the whole class	•	•	•		•	•	•	•	•	•
c to recognise choices they can make, and the difference between right and wrong	•	•	•	•		•	•	•	•	•
d to agree and follow rules for their group and classroom, and to understand how rules help them	•	•	•	•		•	•			
e to recognise that people and other living things have needs, and that they have responsibilities to meet them	•	•		•	•	•	•	•	•	•
g what improves and harms their local, natural and built environments and about some of the ways people look after them	•						•			•
3b to maintain personal hygiene	•	•			•			•		
d about the process of growing from young to old and how people's needs change		•					•			
e the main parts of the body		•				•				
f that all household products, including medicine, can be harmful if not used properly	•	•						•		
4a to recognise how their behaviour affects other people	•	•	•				•	•	•	•
b to listen to other people, and play and work cooperatively	•	•	•	•	•	•	•	•	•	•
c to identify and respect the differences and similarities between people	•	•	•	•	•	•	•	•	•	•
d that family and friends should care for each other	•	•	•			•	•	•	•	•
e that bullying is wrong, there are different types of teasing and bullying, and how to get help to deal with bullying								•	•	

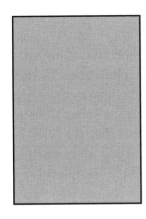

Glossary

This glossary of the dramatic terms used in this book is not necessary to teach the activities in the foregoing chapters since each activity is fully explained in the text. However, a glossary providing explanations of a range of the dramatic approaches used in the book may help those who, having used them in these dramas, wish to plan their own drama sessions.

Conscience alley or thought tunnel

This invites children to examine a moment in the drama in detail. It is employed most effectively when a decision has to be made, or when a decision has already been irrevocably made. Sometimes it requires the children to offer advice to a character, too. Children consider what they or the character might think about the decision and its implications.

The children stand in two lines facing each other about a metre apart. The teacher walks very slowly from one end of the 'alley' to the other. As she does so, she turns to the child to one side and then to the other. They speak aloud a word or line (e.g. to Goldilocks, *'You should leave this cottage'*).

The thought tunnel offers a way of speaking a character's thoughts, rather than offering advice. The character moves through the tunnel in exactly the same way.

Alleys or tunnels can be curved to represent the context, such as a winding path, but straight lines enable children to see and hear each other better.

Discussion in role

Here the teacher is in role as well as the children while they discuss an issue or problem. The conversation is not *about* the characters (e.g. *What do you think frightens him?*) but *between* the characters (e.g. *Do you understand why I am frightened?*). The meeting takes place *as if* the teacher and children are other people in another place; in a fictional context. Discussion in role may be set up as a formal meeting held to sort out problems or discuss plans.

Dramatic construction

We have used this term to describe moments when the children physically 'become' something inanimate. They become a bridge in 'Billy Goats Gruff' (Book 3) and a fish tank in 'Helping at the Pet Shop' (Book 2). It may be used to set the scene for action as in the former, or to introduce terms and understand a structure as in the latter.

Dramatic play

Here children are indulging in imaginative play, but in the context of the shared drama. They may be preparing some food, making a toy or painting a rocket. The action is not controlled by the teacher, but the teacher may wander around among the children asking them about what they are doing as though she, too, is involved in the fiction: *What flavour is your cake going to be? How will you make that? How did you reach to paint that top bit?*

The children have freedom for individual creativity, and are involved in their own worlds, so that one is baking a cake in a kitchen while another is shopping for drinks. High levels of concentration or emotion are not necessary in dramatic play, though of course they may occur. The activity helps to build up belief in the fiction.

Hot seating

The teacher is usually the best person to have in a hot seat since the pressure can be high. The device is helpful as a way to give information to children without being 'the teacher'. The children can ask questions directly to a character in a hot seat to find out whatever they wish to know. This requires them to think of the most appropriate questions and sometimes the best way of asking them. The children may ask as themselves or in role as others in the drama.

Meeting

This highly structured activity engages the teacher and children together in role, gathered for a specific purpose. This may be to hear new information, make plans or discuss strategies. The teacher will usually be the chair or leader at the meeting so that she can order the proceedings and ensure all the children's views are heard. Formal meetings are enhanced by an arrangement of chairs or benches in appropriate rows, and perhaps an agreed action when the chair enters the room. Decisions about pace and procedures will depend upon the context of the meeting.

Narration and narration with mimed action

Teacher narration in drama activities is a useful strategy for setting the scene or moving the action along. It is often a very useful controlling device! The teacher is empowered to dictate particular aspects of the drama. A class working noisily, for example, may hear the teacher narrate, *Gradually, they fell silent. The helpers were too tired to speak.* Narration is also used to excite interest and build tension in the drama (e.g. *No one knew what was inside the bag. Some wondered if it might contain secrets while others felt sure it contained the lost treasure*). It may be used to set the scene (e.g. *The hall was enormous and richly decorated*) and to move the action forward (e.g. *They all packed their bags and started out on the dangerous journey*).

We enjoy drawing the children into narration through mimed action. *The villagers had to climb up over high rocks*, on a journey, for example, would be accompanied by everyone miming climbing over imaginary rocks. It may also be used to help the children to imagine they are all one character (e.g. *She put on her big strong boots, tying the laces tightly. She then put on a heavy coat and did up the buttons, one, two, three and four*). Each child, in his or her own space, will mime the actions as the teacher narrates.

Ritual

Ritual is a repeated procedure that those involved give value to and are familiar with. In drama a ritual is used to give action significance. Any action, no matter how mundane, may be performed in a formal and dignified manner to make the actions seem to matter. Putting items into a picnic basket, for example, by having one child at a time step forward to place an imaginary contribution into the basket announcing what it is, brings about a more serious level of thought to the action and a more exciting atmosphere.

Statementing

Statementing involves the children literally in making statements about a person, event or place in the drama. The statements may be made in a ritualistic manner, with children stepping forward one at a time to give their statement. They may remain frozen in a gesture appropriate to the statement while others make their statements, or they may return to their original place and watch the others. It is a way of involving the children in the construction of events or characters so that they have a sense of ownership.

Still images and still image building

To make still images, children arrange themselves as though they are in a three-dimensional picture, depicting a scene or a particular moment. It creates a frozen moment when we imagine time has stopped, giving us the opportunity to look at it more closely.

Still images may be created by small groups, or by the whole group. They may be created quickly in the count to five, or they may be built one person at a time. This still image-building approach enables children to respond to what others are doing in the still image by placing themselves in a position that relates to another's. A child seeing someone else in an image on a swing in a park may stand behind the swing as though she is pushing it higher.

Storytelling

This activity includes different modes of storytelling. Sometimes the teacher provides narration with pauses that the children fill in. This involves them in the storytelling and makes their contribution part of the whole. At other times storytelling is suggested as a way to involve all the children in reviewing the events of the drama. Here each child takes it in turns to tell a line of the story. Older children may divide into small groups to storytell together.

Teacher in role

The teacher takes the role of someone in the drama. This enables the teacher to work with the children from inside the drama. Additional information may be given through the teacher's role, and questions posed to challenge the children's ideas and assumptions.

Thought tapping

Thought tapping is used in conjunction with mimed activity or most commonly with still images. Once the children are doing either of these, the teacher moves among them and taps them on the shoulder one at a time. She may ask about what the children are doing, about what they are thinking or feeling, or about what they can see or smell or bear from where they are. It invites children to commit further to their roles and to the drama, and to think further about the context. Their contributions become part of the shared understanding of the imaginary place and people. It is a quite controlled activity that gives less vocal individuals their moment.

Whole group improvisation

This activity involves the children and the teacher working together in role. The teacher will have teacher intentions in mind, but the ideas and suggestions offered by the children, and therefore the responses of the teacher, will vary when working with different groups. It is this mode of activity which often generates a high level of concentration and emotional commitment. Unlike dramatic play, the children are all engaged in one world, dealing with the same problem.

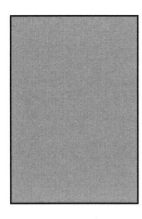

Games

A cleared space is needed for all these games and a circle of chairs is required for 'Fruit Bowl'.

Grandmother's Footsteps

Person **A** faces a wall, or stands with his or her back to the rest of the group. The others stand in a line next to each other all facing **A** back. Their aim is to creep up towards **A** without ever moving when **A** looks around. If they reach **A** before anyone else, they tap him or her on the shoulder and win the game. **A**'s aim is to make sure that no one achieves this.

 A must face away from the others for a few seconds but turn around at regular intervals to try to catch people moving. **A** can vary the time facing the wall so as to turn unexpectedly and catch as many people moving as possible. The others attempt to move only when **A** is facing the wall. If **A** sees them moving or wobbling, he or she calls their name and they must go back to where they started. A may send a few back at one go if they are all moving. The game is over when someone touchs **A**'s shoulder. This is the winner and can take **A**'s place.

 This game is about physical control, concentration and challenge. It creates a building up of tension as people get nearer to **A**.

 A similar game is 'What's the Time Mr Wolf?'

Keeper of the Keys

Person **A** sits blindfolded on a chair in the middle of the space. There is a bunch of keys or jingling object beneath the chair. The others stand at some distance in a wide circle around the chair. Their aim is to get the keys. **A**'s aim is to ensure that the keys remain under the chair.

 Those around the edge must move as quietly as they can towards the chair. If **A** hears any sound, he or she points in the direction of the sound. Whoever is pointed at must move back to the perimeter of the circle and begin again. Whoever is able to grab the keys without being pointed at is the winner and takes the place of person **A**.

 This can also be played with individuals approaching the chair one at a time.

 This game, too, involves physical control and coordination as well as concentration. It may be used with a different item under the chair that is relevant to the drama.

Captain's Coming!

The teacher explains the commands that the children must respond to. They imagine they are on board a large ship/sailing vessel.

'Captain's coming!' means that they all stand still with a straight back and a salute.

'Bombs overhead!' means that they lie on the floor face down with arms and legs straight.

'Scrub the decks!' means that they mime scrubbing the decks.

You can designate directions and include *'Port!'* and *'Starboard'*. You can use a few commands to begin with and build in more as the children get better at remembering and responding quickly.

The teacher or a child calls out the commands and the children get into the appropriate positions as quickly as possible. The last one into the correct position is out. The winner is the person left in at the end. Between commands, the children can move around the space not touching each other. You could play music such as a sea-shanty and turn it down as you call the commands. If the children can dance the hornpipe they may do so between commands!

This is a fun energetic activity. Children have to be ready to respond very quickly to instructions so it does require concentration. It encourages speedy reactions. You can adapt the game for different contexts. *'Teacher's coming!'* in a school-based drama might generate commands such as *'Line up'* and *'Sit in a circle'*. The children can make up commands for the game.

Fruit Bowl

The children sit on chairs in a circle. There should be no empty chairs. Each child is allocated one of three names (e.g. apple, mango or banana). A caller stands in the middle of the circle and calls out one of the fruits (e.g. mango), and all the mangoes have to leave their seats and rush to find another chair to sit on. The caller's aim is to sit on a chair too. Whoever is left without a chair is the next caller. If 'Fruit Bowl' is called, everyone has to leave their chairs and find another. Players are not allowed to return to the chairs they have just vacated. When their fruit is called they must find new chairs. The aim for everybody is to ensure they are sitting on a chair.

This game may be adapted to introduce different names, such as fish in the drama 'Under the Sea' (Book 2), animals in 'Helping at the Pet Shop' (Book 2) or new vocabulary such as doctors' equipment in 'The Health Centre' (Book 1). The game may also be used to set up the context of where the drama will take place. Any names, terms or even descriptive words may be used. This is a fun way to introduce new or difficult vocabulary to children. New words introduced in the game will soon become familiar.

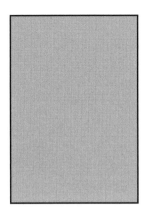

Suggestions for further reading

This is not a comprehensive list. There are many useful books available about drama in education and activities for the early years. We feel that the following books complement this series.

Ackroyd, J. (ed.) (2000) *Literacy Alive*, London: Hodder & Stoughton.

Ackroyd, J. and Boulton, J. (2001) *Drama Lessons for Five to Eleven-Year-Olds*, London: David Fulton.

Aldridge, M. (2003) *Meeting the Early Learning Goals through Role Play*, London: David Fulton.

Beetlestone, F. (1998) *Creative Children, Imaginative Teaching*, Buckingham: The Open University Press.

Bolton, G. (1984) *Drama as Education*, London: Longman.

Bolton, G. (1992) *New Perspectives on Classroom Drama*, London: Simon & Schuster Educational.

Booth, D. (1994) *Story Drama*, Markham: Pembroke.

Booth, D. (2002) *Even Hockey Players Read*, Markham: Pembroke.

Bowell, P. and Heap, B. (2001) *Planning Process Drama*, London: David Fulton.

Clipson-Boyles, S. (1999) *Drama in the Primary Classroom*, London: David Fulton.

Drake, J. (2003) *Organising Play in the Early Years*, London: David Fulton.

Emblen, V. and Helen, S. (1992) *Learning Through Story*, Leamington Spa: Scholastic Press.

Fleming, M. (1994) *Starting Drama Teaching*, London: David Fulton.

Kempe, A. and Holroyd, J. (2003) *Speaking, Listening and Drama*, London: David Fulton.

Miller, C. and Saxton, J. (2004) *Into the Story: Language in Action Through Drama*, New Hampshire: Heinemann.

Mudd, S. and Mason, H. (1993) *Tales for Topics: Linking Favourite Stories with Popular Topics for Children Aged Five to Nine*, Twickenham: Belair Publications.

Neelands, J. (1992) *Learning Through Imagined Experience*, London: Hodder & Stoughton.

Neelands, J. and Goode, T. (2000) *Structuring Drama Work, Second Edition*, London: Hodder & Stoughton.

O'Neill, C. (1995) *Drama Worlds*, London: Heinemann.

Toye, N. and Prendiville, F. (2000) *Drama and Traditional Story for the Early Years*, London: Routledge/Falmer.

Winston, J. (2000) *Drama, Literacy and Moral Education 5–11*, London: David Fulton.

Winston, J. and Tandy, M. (2002) *Beginning Drama*, London: David Fulton.

Ready, Steady, Play!

Guaranteed fun for children and practitioners alike, the Ready Steady Play! series provides lively and stimulating activities for children.

Each book focuses on one specific aspect of play offering clear and detailed guidance on how to plan and enjoy wonderful play experiences with minimum fuss and maximum success.

Available from September 2004!

Each book in the Ready, Steady, Play! series includes advice on:

- How to prepare the children and the play space
- What equipment and materials are needed
- How much time is needed to prepare and carry out the activity
- How many staff required
- How to communicate with parents and colleagues

Early years practitioners and students on early years courses and parents looking for simple, excellent ideas for creative play will love these books!

Ready, Steady Play! helps you to:

- Develop activities easily, using suggested guidelines
- Ensure that health and safety issues are taken into account
- Plan play that links to the early years curriculum
- Broaden your understanding of early years issues

David Fulton Publishers

Order Form

Qty	ISBN	Title	Price	Subtotal
	1-84312-148-4	Books, Stories and Puppets	£12.00	
	1-84312-098-4	Construction	£12.00	
	1-84312-076-3	Creativity	£12.00	
	1-84312-267-7	Displays and Interest Tables	£12.00	
	1-84312-101-8	Festivals	£12.00	
	1-84312-100-X	Food and Cooking	£12.00	
	1-84312-276-6	Music and Singing	£12.00	
	1-84312-114-X	Nature, Living and Growing	£12.00	
	1-84312-099-2	Play Using Natural Materials	£12.00	
	1-84312-147-6	Role Play	£12.00	
	1-84312-204-9	David Fulton 2004 catalogue	FREE	
			P&P	
			Total	

Postage and Packing: FREE to schools and LEAs. £2.50 for orders to private addresses. Prices and publication dates are subject to change

Please complete delivery details:

NAME: ....

ADDRESS: ....

....

POSTCODE: .... TEL: ....

EMAIL: ....

☐ **Please invoice** (applicable to schools, LEAs and other institutions). *Invoices will be sent from our distributor.*

☐ **I enclose a cheque** payable to *David Fulton Publishers Ltd.* (*include postage & packing*)

☐ **Please charge to my credit card** (we accept all major credit cards including switch).

Credit Card No:

☐☐☐☐☐☐☐☐☐☐☐☐

☐☐☐☐☐☐☐

Exp. Date: ☐☐☐☐

(Switch customers only)

Valid from: ☐☐☐☐   Issue no: ☐

FREE Postage and Packing to Schools and LEAs!

Send your order to: Harper Collins Publishers • Customer Service Centre • Westerhill Road • Bishopbriggs Glasgow • G64 2QT • Tel: 0870 787 1721 • Fax: 0870 787 1723 • www.fultonpublishers.co.uk

Please quote ref. DF0009 on your order